D1245763

GETTING
THINGS
DONE
Eva
Burrows

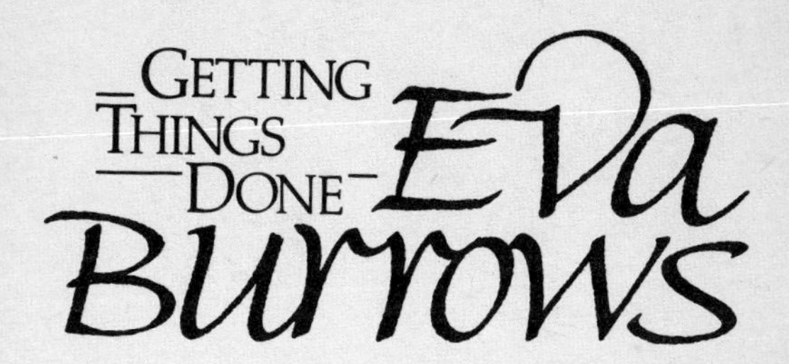

A BIOGRAPHY

WENDY GREEN

Marshall
Pickering

Acknowledgement is due to all the people who have made this book possible.

Marshall Morgan and Scott
Marshall Pickering
3 Beggarwood Lane, Basingstoke,
Hants RG23 7LP, UK

Copyright © 1988 Wendy Green

First published in 1988 by
Marshall Morgan and Scott Publications Ltd.
Part of the Marshall Pickering Holdings Group

A subsidiary of the Zondervan Corporation

All rights reserved. No part of this publication may be reproduced, stored in a retrieval system, or transmitted, in any form or by any means, electronic, mechanical, photocopying, recording or otherwise, without the prior permission, in writing, of the publisher.

British Library CIP Data
Burrows, Eva
Getting things done.
1. Salvation Army. Burrows, Eva
I. Title II. Green, Wendy
267'.15'0924

ISBN: 0 551 01713 9

Text set in Baskerville by The Ikthos Studios,
Chute Forest, Andover, Hampshire.

Printed and bound in Great Britain by
Cox & Wyman Ltd, Reading

Getting Things Done

CHAPTER ONE

It was Sunday morning. Father was conducting 'knee drill', the early morning prayer meeting, in the hall next to the house. Mother was in bed, sick. Ten-year-old Joyce was preparing breakfast for the family. Suddenly the lusty cry of a new-born baby sounded from the front bedroom. Joyce's heart sank.

'Oh no. Not another baby. We have enough.' It was September 15th, 1929. Already six children and the two adults were cramped into the Salvation Army quarters at Tighes Hill, Newcastle, a mining town in Eastern Australia. Captain and Mrs Burrows were both full-time officers and totally involved in the life of the busy corps. Joyce, as the oldest daughter living at home, shared a fair burden of the domestic responsibility. A new baby would only add to her workload. Why couldn't she live with granny and grandpa, and help care for them, like Dorothy the sister who was a couple of years older?

Captain Burrows seems to have greeted the arrival of the new baby with an equal lack of enthusiasm. When the midwife interrupted the prayers to inform him he had another daughter he replied tersely, 'I'll attend to it all when I've finished here.'

Joyce wisely decided to take her three smallest charges around the block to get away from the trauma, and to give herself chance to adjust to the idea. Within minutes father returned home, lifted the new-born baby in his arms, and redeemed himself somewhat by pronouncing, 'I dedicate this child to the glory of God and the salvation of the world.'

The baby was named Eva Evangeline after her mother's sister, Eva, and Evangeline Booth, the fiery red-haired daughter of William Booth, the founder of the Salvation Army. Captain Burrows obviously had great expectations for his new offspring.

His sincerity was in keeping with Army tradition. Total commitment had characterised Salvation Army families from the beginning. William Booth and his wife, Catherine, had set the pattern. When they started their 'mission' amongst the poor and destitute of the great cities of Britain they already had six children. Each of the children, especially the eldest, Bramwell, were involved with the work from an early age. Booth's awareness that 'nobody gets a blessing when they have cold feet' meant that Bramwell was in charge of heating and supplying five centres where the poor could buy a cheap lunch by the time he was sixteen. Fifteen years later when William saw scores of homeless men sleeping on the streets it was Bramwell he commanded, 'Go and do something'.
the money and made sure his father's ideas for the new organisation, named The Salvation Army, in 1878, were implemented. Within months of his marriage his wife, Florence, was leader of the women's social services. Her main work was centred at a refuge for prostitutes and the women under her charge became used to the sight of her arriving with the latest member of her growing family in her arms. The baby would be handed into the care of one of her 'other family', or placed in a basket or drawer to sleep. Unlike many leisured women of the middle and upper classes she combined a 'career' with her role of wife and homemaker. Bramwell, like his father, found the Army took the main portion of his time and concern. Years later his eldest daughter Catherine commented, 'The Army came first and the position was accepted by all of us as part of the existing order.'

With William's death in 1912 a sealed envelope announced, as was expected, that he nominated Bramwell as his successor. For a decade and a half Bramwell served the movement faithfully but as he approached his seventies speculation began to grow about who was to follow him. The Salvation Army had grown from a small backstreet mission in the East End of London to an international organisation. Its social and evangelistic outposts in numerous countries were staffed by many competent officers. In 1927 his sister Evangeline presented a 'reasoned memorandum' suggesting that it would be wise to estab-lish a different method of appointing the next General. Bramwell resisted any such idea, even though his health was deteriorating. His last public act was to lay the cornerstone of a new international training college in memory of his father on May 10th, 1928. In November a meeting of a decision-making body known as the High Council was called. They met on January 8th, 1929 and a new General was elected by mid-February. Bramwell died that June, three months before Eva Burrows was born. Despite the fact that air travel and the new-fangled wireless were in their infancy and television still in the experimental stages, the news must have reached the far corners of the Salvation Army empire eventually. Never-theless the day-to-day concerns of the corps and family must have seemed far more pressing issues to the Burrows family than political manoeuvrings in the Salvation Army hierachy half a world away.

Even the agitations of the women's movement would have warranted little more than a raised eyebrow from a lass in a Salvation Army bonnet that had to be strong enough to protect the head of the wearer from brick bats and other missiles. The 'Hallelujah lasses' had been used to raising their own voices in protest and employing some fairly dramatic methods to attract attention from the time Catherine Booth took up the cudgels on behalf of women in the early days of the movement. Single women had been trained and commissioned as officers from 1880 when colleges for both sexes had been established.

However, in the 1920s it was still unusual for a married couple to be accepted for training. Robert and Ella Burrows were not only married, they already had three small children when they felt the compulsion to enter the ministry. Maybe the fact that a new college had recently been opened in Sydney meant there were more vacancies. More likely Robert and Ella were not easily dissuaded. Whatever the reasons and after some soul searching they sold their home and entered college in 1921, making the best arrangements they could for the children.

Dorothy, the eldest, went to the maternal grandparents, where she stayed for a number of years. Joyce and Beverley, the first boy, were placed in a Salvation Army children's home, 'The Fold'. The training lasted only four months, but during that time the young mother was only able to spend one precious afternoon a week with her babies.

Soon after the Burrows' appointment to a suburban corps, Haberfield, in Sydney, a second son, Walter Livingstone, was born. The inspiration for his second name came not from the famous missionary and explorer, but the street in Sydney where his parents' college had been situated. They were so delighted to have had the opportunity for training, whatever the personal cost. Although the training was short the couple made excellent officers, full of zeal and compassion. They were not ones for putting their hand to the plough then looking back. When he emigrated to Australia at the age of nineteen Robert Burrows was little more than an irreligious rebel. In London he had joined gangs who had thrown rotten tomatoes, eggs or whatever was at hand into Salvation Army meetings. In Australia he was more hesitant. A young Salvation Army lassie with black curly hair, brown eyes and a peaches and cream complexion had caught his eye. Nudging his mate as they strolled past an open air meeting at Murwillumbah, New South Wales, he announced, 'See that girl there. I'm going to marry her'.

His mate was never to know that this could be anything

more than wishful thinking. Some weeks later he was sleeping off the effects of alcohol beside the Tweed River when he rolled down the bank, into the river, and was drowned. Robert, at a loss, went on a drinking spree in which he spent most of the savings he had accumulated during his first few months in the new country. Despite the effects of the drink he paused to listen at another of the meetings, heard a testimony from a young man who later turned out to be Ella's brother, and was converted.

His knowledge of the Bible was minimal but he soon made up for it. He obtained a job in the town on a delivery cart, the old-fashioned horse and dray, and memorised Salvation Army doctrine, and verses from the Bible as he drove the cart. Quite what the inhabitants made of that is perhaps left buried in history but it must have impressed Ella for they were married in 1918.

Although Ella was a third generation Salvationist her commitment was as strong as her husband's. It needed to be, with a different corps every couple of years once they became officers and a new baby born every eighteen months or so. By the time Eva was born the family went down in 'steps and stairs'. There were the two eldest girls, Dorothy and Joyce, then four boys, Beverley, Walter, Robert and Bramwell, and another girl Elizabeth, who was always known as Betty. The birth of Eva and the arrival of Margaret a couple of years later completed the family.

CHAPTER TWO

When Eva was three years old she was taken by train to the city. Mrs Burrows had baby Margaret in her arms, Joyce had Eva by the hand. Eva looked a picture. Mrs Burrows had made her a red coat with fur on the collar and cuffs and it suited her dark hair and huge brown eyes perfectly.

They went into a large department store with doorways opening into two main streets, Queen Street and Adelaide Street. At a certain counter Mrs Burrows needed Joyce's opinion on some purchases. Joyce let go of Eva's hand for a second in order to see better. The next thing they knew she had vanished.

Joyce raced through the store, searching desperately. At the Queen Street entrance she caught a glimpse of a red-clad figure running as fast as her legs would carry her to keep up with the woman who was taking her away. Joyce raced down the road despite the crowds and snatched the child away from the would-be thief.

Family prayers must have been said with particular fervour that night but it wasn't only the dramatic episode that drove Ella Burrows to her knees. Eva had been born the year of the Wall Street crash. The harsh years of the Depression were causing everyone to tighten their belts. By now the 'peaches and cream' teenager was in her forties, and grey haired, with nine children to feed and clothe.

How they coped with no child benefit or social security back up says a great deal for their determination and the sacrifices that had to be made by them all. Robert Burrows' wages were often less than ten shillings a week. Fortunately both parents were experts at managing money; Robert at saving , when and if there was anything to save; Ella at making the housekeeping stretch twice as far as anyone else. She always had an eye for a bargain and was very astute in her shopping. Even so there were times when the money just would not stretch far enough.

Queensland has a warm tropical climate and going barefoot was quite common even for the boys but some form of footwear was needed on occasion. Each child had one pair of all-purpose shoes but often there was little more than the uppers remaining. The gospels commend faith the size of a grain of mustard seed. Ella Burrows' faith was giant size, and it was rewarded. She was closing the church door one evening after the service when an unknown benefactor pushed an envelope through the gap into her hand. On the outside was written 'MONEY FOR SHOES'.

Salvation Army officers did not receive a salary. They were given an allowance, depending on their need and what was available, which was precious little in the Depression. Fortunately some soldiers felt real responsibility for their officers and often gave gifts in kind if they didn't have any spare cash. Another anonymous donor regularly left a sugar bag full of food on the Burrows' front verandah. Out of the bag would roll a large cabbage, a leg of mutton, potatoes, Granny Smith apples and some 'goodies' for the excited children.

Toys were few and far between. The children improvised. Pieces of pine from apple cases became cricket bats, tennis rackets or hockey sticks and gave them endless hours of pleasure. Beds were almost as primitive. A couple of double spring matresses were placed across half a dozen apple cases. On top of this was an old worn fibre mattress, and into each bed went four boys or four girls. The springs sagged in the middle and before night was over all four bodies were entangled in a heap in the middle.

Washing was done by hand. The clothes were boiled in a copper over a wood fire, rubbed up and down on a wash board, then squeezed through a hand-turned mangle. Garments were usually 'make do and mend'. Even in the worst years of the Depression there were still people wealthy enough to give their cast-offs to the poor, and they didn't come much poorer than a Salvation Army officer's family. Joyce and her mother would wash, unpick, iron and re-cut articles from the poor box, making them into garments which their original owners would have been hard pressed to recognise. Legs were cut from trousers to make jackets for the boys or skirts for the girls, and all kinds of things would be 'adjusted' to fit the next member of the family. No fancy patterns were necessary. Mrs Burrows learnt the hard way. With four boys to keep in trousers she bought a pair of pants from the store, unpicked them to see how they were put together, cut a pattern from the pieces and never looked back. Many of Captain Burrows' uniforms were made by her. So were the boys' band uniforms and all the girls' clothing. Joyce became her 'right hand', sitting on the stool beside her sewing. She was packed off to bed by midnight but Mrs Burrows often worked patiently on till the early hours of the morning. When Eva was five the girls had their photograph taken with Eva proudly wearing 'a very nice dress with some smocking across it', which Joyce had made by hand.

The family car, an old Rugby, was kept going with similar improvisation. Donated by a kind benefactor at some stage and affectionately known as 'the old bomb', it always seemed to get them to country open airs and cottage meetings but took exception to a trip to Sydney for a Congress. Captain and Mrs Burrows were well under way when the car broke down, leaving them stranded on the mountain side, with no garages or help for miles around. Ever-resourceful Ella had already put her imagination to good use by tying a suitcase with an old electric cord when no strap was to be found. That piece of cord contained the very wire that could be used to fix the car.

There were few holidays, or trips to the famous surf of the Australian beaches, until friends of the family lent them a house by the sea in later years.

'We lived a very spartan life,' says Eva, 'but I can't ever remember thinking other kids had a lot, and we hadn't. I must have been quite content and happy. My mother said she never was without. God seemed always to supply our needs. The family say I take after my mother a great deal in that she could make do and be happy. She had a great love for her children and we all loved her intensely.'

Eva attributes her education and training for officership to her mother's self giving and determination. Mrs Burrows nursed Betty through a dangerous illness when the doctor had given up hope on her. One of the brothers was conscious of his mother's presence in stressful situations for years afterwards and Joyce speaks of her 'strong influence on each of our lives'.

She was the focal point. Wife, mother, minister, an immaculate homemaker. Clean and well organised, she could conjure up the best with the poorest ingredients. Lollies, jams, pickles, cakes, pies. Scones were her speciality and light as floss. Eva enjoyed 'dampers', a kind of bread without yeast made by the swagmen on their wanderings. There was nothing fancy, just simple, basic home cooking, which frequently had to stretch to include the destitute people Ella would invite to share the family's meals.

At one time the family lived next door to a prostitute, an older woman who was 'rather fat and ungainly and sloppy looking'. Rather than criticising, or poking fun at her, like the other neighbours, Ella Burrows took a special interest in her, handing her food she had cooked, things she had made. Slowly, imperceptibly, Mrs Burrows' influence began to draw out the woman's hidden qualities until one day she shocked the neighbourhood in a different way: by appearing decently dressed, and attending the women's meeting.

On top of all this Ella was fully involved as a corps officer, leading open air meetings, visiting, distributing the magazine *War Cry* round the public houses, and preaching. She used a lot of illustration in her sermons, often taking stories from Rita Snowden's books or the Bible to relate Christian truth to everyday experience.

She was greatly loved by all who knew her and no matter how tired she felt or how troublesome people might be her children never heard her complain. To them she appeared patient, tolerant, loving. Not with a wishy-washy kind of love, but with the strong love that has no favourites, doesn't pamper or fuss, but in which children can feel secure. Despite the volume of sheer hard physical slog there must have been with no vacuum cleaners, washing machines, electric mixers or all the other electronic gadgetry which have eased the burden of housework considerably Eva has no recollection of her mother getting uptight or tense. When the going was tough Ella Burrows relied on a power beyond her own. Her favourite verse of scripture was 'I will lift up mine eyes unto the hills, from whence cometh my help. My help cometh from the Lord.' (Psalm 121, verse 1, AV).

She also had a fair amount of assistance from the older children. They had a disciplined system, and Captain Burrows ruled the household with military precision. The children were his 'rookie soldiers'. There was a roster on the kitchen wall. Dorothy do ironing. Joyce do washing up. Beverley polish silver. Walter rake yard. Robert run messages. Eva somehow managed to escape. Either because she was at the bottom end of the family, or because she always had a book to study. None of the family can ever recall Eva being domesticated, though they knew only too well the consequences of jobs not done. As was quite normal in those days Robert Burrows kept a strap hanging on a hook at the end of the dining table. One look from their father and the children got the message. There was no lack of love, but there were limits, and the children were expected to stick to them. Respect for their seniors was near the top of the list . . . however high or humble they might be. 'Obedience was number one priority,' Joyce recollects, 'and the respect and love we had for our parents and for one another forced us into a very successful household.'

When Joyce was a teenager Commissioner Charles Duncan came to inspect the corps, and his words in one of the public meetings stuck in her memory: 'I have never been in such a well ordered home.' As well as being a strict disciplinarian Captain Burrows was a good administrator and a born leader. In such a big household there needed to be some organisation and control so father provided the discipline and mother tempered it with mercy. Nor was it all work.There was lots of fun and laughter. With no television to distract them the family formed their own orchestra, and often visited jails for services and concerts. Captain Burrows played the violin, Mrs Burrows and Joyce had guitars, Beverley flexed his muscles on the piano accordion, Walter had a saxophone. The rest joined in with ukuleles, tambourines, whatever they could manage.All the children were expected to learn an instrument as they became old enough and were taught by talented Salvationists free of charge. They were like cogs working together, fitting into place when and where they were needed. Each had a position and a purpose, and a valued part to play.

CHAPTER THREE

Captain Burrows may have been the head of the household but Mrs Burrows was definitely the heart. Joyce used to have terrible nightmares about what would happen to 'all the little children' if God did not answer her prayers to keep mother 'safe and well and strong'. Similar thoughts must have crossed Robert Burrows' mind at times for he had a 'tremendous burden and task ' which would have been very difficult to accomplish unaided.

Both parents were always at the beck and call of the general public. The poor, sick, bereaved, came knocking at the door. There were problems to sort out in the church, pastoral needs, finance, administration, weeknight meetings, women's meetings, children's work. People had to be visited at home and in hospital. Sunday meant several meetings and sermons to prepare. Captain Burrows needed complete silence for this task. Mother had to struggle on with nine children making a terrible din, and almost drowning out her powers of concentration.

Saturday night must have been pandemonium with everybody needing their turn in the washtub. Sunday morning was hardly less hectic. The boys had to be coaxed into blazers and skull caps. Three little girls had to be dressed smartly with ribbons in their well-brushed hair.

The Burrows children were expected to be examples to the other youngsters in the corps, and had to sit in the front seats of any hall they attended, where Captain Burrows could keep his eagle eye on them. The small ones were allowed a mat or blanket on the floor where they curled up if they felt sleepy. In the Salvation Army the emphasis is very much on participation and from an early age the children were encouraged to sing, play, read the lesson, play in the band or timbrel group. When they were older at least two of them preached the sermon when the need arose.

Sunday started with 'knee drill', the early morning prayer meeting at 7am. The older ones took turns to accompany their father, then it was all hands on deck getting breakfast and everyone ready for ten o'clock Sunday School. Joyce then had the task of making sure each child was in place for the morning 'Holiness' meeting, while Captain and Mrs Burrows welcomed people as they arrived.

After the morning service there was a brisk walk home for lunch which had been prepared and cooked on the Saturday. Stew or soup was followed by pumpkin, or 'Grammar' pie, with a tiny tin of cream diluted with milk. Then it was back to the hall for afternoon Sunday School, and a public praise meeting. Again the children did their bit to ensure that everything went smoothly. From the ages of nine or ten they distributed magazines and helped to hand out the Sunday School 'tickets', picture cards of birds or flowers with a short text from the Bible. By the time she was fifteen Joyce was acting as unpaid assistant lieutenant, doing a weekly round of shops who subscribed to the corps and 'pub booming', calling at pubs with an armful of the Army magazine *War Cry* and her collecting box.

Sunday tea was bread and dripping sprinkled with salt and pepper, one of mum's scones, and a piece of jam tart with twisty squiggles of pastry on top. When the children were young 'big sister' was delegated to get the smaller ones ready for bed while her mother shared the leadership of the evening services. Joyce told the children fairy stories or Bible stories and they sang Army songs and choruses. Then each child had to be taught to say their prayers. When Captain and Mrs Burrows came home exhausted after their demanding day all the children would be sound asleep.

As they got older they accompanied their parents in the evening too, running as fast as they could go for fear of being late for the six o'clock open air meeting in one of the streets. Discipline was the order of the day in the corps as well as in the house. Woebetide anyone who was untidy or out of step on one of the marches. Half past seven brought the grand finale, the evening or 'Salvation' meeting. This would end with a 'Hallelujah' wind-up, or glory march where someone would take the flag and lead a march round the hall to songs of victory and praise. Then with school looming ominously on the next day's horizon there was a stampede home to see who could be first in bed.

If the message didn't sink in on a Sunday a range of weeknight meetings reinforced it. There was Sunbeams, Chums, Corps Cadets, Guards, Scouts and Bible class, according to age and interest. Those with musical talent had band or singing practice. Eva remembers enjoying the music and playing the tambourine from when she was a small girl. 'Even going out to the open air services. We don't wait till we're eighteen. We believe in child conversion.' Joyce dates her own conversion to the age of eight when she made her pledge and vows in the Sunbeams, an organisation similar to Brownies but with slightly more spiritual content. Eva recollects making a commitment to Christ when she became a junior soldier. Kneeling at the 'mercy seat', a bench at the front of the hall where people are called in penitence and dedication, was also a regular part of their experience.

There were two more open airs during the week and somewhere in between all this activity the children had homework to complete. All the Burrows children were 'born energetic', a characteristic they seem to have inherited from their parents. It was unheard of for Captain and Mrs Burrows to take even half a day off during their ministry, but there were times when the older children were close to tears over their exercise books. There was just so much to be crammed into each short day. Apparently 'The twentieth century Salvationist is an activist . . . he is happiest when he is doing something.' *(Booth's Drum)*

Ella and Robert Burrows were perfect examples. The children simply followed in their footsteps. For the older ones this meant baby minding, potato peeling, biscuit baking. Often all at the same time. The younger ones had simpler jobs, like delivering copies of the *War Cry* to corps members who had failed to show up for service on Sunday. It was God first, people next and self last. Or 'love expressed in service'.

'We were always doing some little task,' says Eva. 'My father loved the Army. He lived for it. We have a colloquial expression "army barmy". It meant such a transformation in his life, a whole new community and way of living.'

When Robert Burrows first became a Christian he had been working on a banana plantation, but some time after his conversion a Salvationist family gave him work on their dairy farm. He ate his meals with them, and couldn't believe his eyes when he saw them saying grace. It was the first time in his life he had seen anyone praying in their house.

His grandfather had been a British general in the Indian Army but Robert had been fatherless from the age of seven when his father was attacked by a gang of hooligans in Fleet Street, London, and died shortly afterwards. Although there were aunts and uncles on the London stage somehow over the years the contact was lost and never re-established.

Great-great grandfather was a descendant of the Guthrie clan in Scotland. When he died his wife re-married and the children took the new family name, Burrows. Robert himself had been born in Dundee in Scotland, and by a strange coincidence Ella was also born in Dundee, several thousand miles away in New South Wales, Australia. Her family history is equally dramatic and could almost have come straight out of the pages of a Barbara Cartland novel.

Her great grandfather, Henry John Dutton, was a Baptist missionary who sailed from England for Jamaica in 1839. His young wife went with him despite being three months pregnant. Before they were out of the English channel a severe storm washed a man overboard and left Mrs Dutton so ill she had to be taken ashore in a pilot boat when the storm dropped. She returned to her parents in Stepney in the East End of London where she died soon after giving birth to a baby daughter in June 1840. Mr Dutton reached Jamaica safely where he took charge of Bethany mission, Clarksville. After his wife's death he married a Miss Drayton who had gone to Jamaica as a single woman missionary teacher. In 1843 he returned to England and took his little daughter back to Jamaica to join the rest of the family. He died three years later in November 1846. His widow and children returned to England and later emigrated to Australia where one of the daughters, Maria Louisa, made a good marriage. Her husband, John Robert Chapple, had arrived in Australia from Devonshire, England, in 1848 at the age of ten. By 1851 the family owned forty thousand acres of land, grazing ten thousand sheep and six thousand lambs. John built the family home, Devon house or 'Chapple mansions', a two-storey brick house in 1864. Here, he and his wife entertained vice-regal parties, governors and other influential Australians, serving them with table wines from their own large cellar. When their daughter, another Maria, joined the Salvation Army she was disinherited. Her Salvation Army journals were seen as 'tools of the devil' and dropped with silver tongs into the flames in a huge log fireplace.

Described as 'quiet, genteel and beautiful – a real aristocrat' Maria can only have compounded her family's displeasure when she eloped with a volatile Irish sheep shearer. In his early days he had been clerk of the race-course, but is more well known as the fiery Salvationist he became after his conversion. Third and fourth generations still talk of Adam Watson, who would not allow any of his six children to drive, bus or tram on the sabbath. He would pace the floor at meetings, pleading 'Lord save souls' and leap over the seats shouting 'Glory' when he saw an answer to his prayers. Two of his daughters, Ella and her sister Eva, became Salvation Army officers and of his thirty three grandchildren some are ministers in the free churches, most are Salvationists and one is the General. The combination of fire and family probably account for the striking personalities of Ella Burrows and her daughter. Even as a child Eva is described as bright eyed, full of life, the apple of everybody's eye. She only remembers her mother when she was already grey-haired, but she still thought of her as beautiful, stately.

'She had a certain style about her,' she says. 'I remember once a woman said to me "Your mother is a real lady". She seemed to have a natural gift of dignity.'

That she could retain it through the tough years of the Depression with no outside help and very little money is remarkable. What is more several of the children seem to have inherited her command and confidence, with Eva receiving a double portion.

As a small child Eva was allowed to sit on a little stool next to the pianist at the Maryborough corps, where she would sing and clap during the meeting. Her first public appearance was at the local eisteddfod at the age of four. Joyce had made her a mauve embroidered organza frock salvaged as usual from the poor box. Joyce was to recite a monologue but she was always a victim of acute nerves and at fifteen was very self conscious. Eva took to it like a duck to water. She stood up with total aplomb, and carried off first prize for her rendering of a 'Purple Pussycat'.

To Joyce's eyes it seemed she 'Always had an abundance of confidence. She seemed to fear no one. She knew exactly what she wanted, and where she wanted to go.'

During that same year Commissioner McKenzie, or 'Fighting Mac', visited the Burrows' home. Known throughout the Army world for his outstanding service as a chaplain in the First World War he was held in great affection and esteem. It was a tremendous honour for the Burrows children to be introduced one by one to this famous and huge framed man. Finally it was Eva's turn. Placing his large hand on her head he looked at her mother. 'Mrs Burrows,' he pronounced, 'one day we will have another Evangeline in this little girl.'

The family took note. 'Another little Eva' they teased long before the small child knew what they were talking about. Even when the famous Evangeline, who was elected first woman General of the Salvation Army in 1934, visited Australia when Eva was six or seven Eva failed to appreciate why everyone was making such a fuss. The family were living in the small town of Gympie. The General was visiting the Congress in Brisbane several hundred miles away. Somehow the whole family managed to make it to Brisbane where Captain Burrows was given the important job of looking after the General's flag. The flag has always been a symbol of the militant faith of the Salvation Army and in the early days of the movement invariably became the main target for the larrikins or hoodlums who did their best to destroy the marches and meetings. General Eva's flag had special significance. She had a strong sense of the dramatic, and could use it to good effect when occasion demanded. What is more it had gold tassles, a feature only found in America, nowhere else in the Salvation Army world. The young Eva's attention was rivetted though Evangeline's famous oratory went straight over her head. She knew vaguely there was a wonderful person everyone was talking about, but who could be more wonderful to a wide-eyed seven year old than the sight of their own father guarding a flag with gold tassles?

CHAPTER FOUR

Despite various indications that Eva was a 'special person' from fairly early on, the rough and tumble of a large family ensured that it didn't turn her head. With one sister slightly older and another two years younger there were real female 'spats' at times with the sisters fighting like young lion cubs. The volatile temperament of the Irish sheep shearer would flash out but it was soon over. With love and forgiveness key words in the Christian gospel, no one held grudges for long.

There was very little envy either, maybe because they were all talented in their own ways, and Captain and Mrs Burrows had the wisdom not to show favouritism. Working on the theory 'Your greatest critics are those of your own household', they would often hold a critical session after a meal. Even the adults were not allowed to escape. Quite which faults of Eva's came under condemnation is unclear but the family pet name for her was 'Draughty'. Whereas the other girls were much gentler in their movements, light and soft, almost dainty, Eva did everything with flair and gusto. When the others saw her heading for home after the latest sports or debating session they would say 'Look out. Here comes Draughty now'. She was always leading and doing things, an extrovert, outgoing. It must have been a considerable advantage when faced with the numerous moves the children had to make in their formative years. Their average stay in a corps was only two years. Most of the children went to at least ten schools, though Eva only managed to notch up eight. There was

Maryborough, Gympie, Fortitude Valley, Albion, Windsor, Wooloongabba, New Farm and finally Brisbane State High School.

Most people have vivid memories of their first day at school and their childhood home. Not Eva. There were too many. The Burrows family were putting into practice the Army policy of 'itinerants for God'. They had no house of their own; only married quarters supplied and furnished by the Army. Even so, with eleven members of the family moving was a massive exercise. Captain Burrows kept three or four huge pine crates, which seemed big enough to pack all nine children, and freight them off to their new home. Into those crates would go clothes, shoes,the occasional toy, school books, Captain and Mrs Burrows' books which they used for sermon preparation, a typewriter and the musical instruments.

According to Eva the children identified with their parents' commitment so there were few grumbles. 'We were always quite excited when the move came. We'd look forward. We didn't say "Oh no,we're leaving our friends. We can't go.'

Being part of a ready-made community must have eased the transitions enormously, for Eva's predominant memory of childhood is not one of upheaval but of 'being happy'. To her, people were more important than places: the young people's sergeant major in charge of the Sunday School who did 'everything well'; teachers at school and Sunday School; Miss Coe, Miss Cooper, Mr Adsett, 'shining people' who seemed to have a kind of glow, a quality of goodness which Eva found very attractive. She admired them, and they inspired, encouraged, and had affection for her.

Eva has always had a special relationship with Margaret, the younger, quieter sister but the ones at the top of the family are also high in her esteem. Joyce was loved for the way she helped 'mother' them and Beverley, the eldest boy, was another of her heroes. He also had a great deal of ability, but like all the older ones had to leave school and go out to work to help support the family once he reached the end of primary school.

In that sense the younger girls were favoured. Most of the older children would have liked to continue their education but it was just not possible financially. There were only two State High Schools in Brisbane. If you came from a poor family the only way you could get secondary education was by gaining a scholarship. With so many moves the education of the Burrows children had been badly disrupted. All the older ones were put back a grade when they moved to Queensland. Only Eva and Margaret made the important transition to secondary school at the age of thirteen or fourteen. Yet there were no sour grapes. Only pride in their achievement, and the present of a bike from brother Beverley when Eva passed her scholarship exams.

It was not until they moved to Brisbane that life became settled enough for a house to hold much significance. It was a Queensland house, built on stilts to allow the air to circulate beneath, and had an enclosed verandah halfway round one side. A central corridor opened onto bedrooms on one side, and on the other side there was a sitting room with a piano and a dining room with solid antique furniture and an oil painting of the owner. Across the back of the house was a kitchen, a bathroom and a big breakfast room with steps leading down to the back garden.

The house was situated in the suburb of Windsor, and the two youngest girls walked to Windsor Primary school each day. The school was in ten acres of ground with terraced playing fields, basket and netball courts, a tennis court and a swimming pool. It was here that Mr Adsett, one of Eva's 'shining people', taught his class of talented youngsters, several of whom passed the scholarship exam. But the shadows that were deepening over Europe were reaching out to 'change everything' in lives across the world, and the Burrows family were to be no exception. The house they lived in belonged to a German lady, a Miss Wacker, who had been home in her own country when war broke out and was unable to return. The night war was declared Mrs Burrows broke down in tears. Joyce tried to comfort her, assuring her that none of the boys would have to go. Of course they did. They even put their ages forward by a year, unknown to their parents, when they enlisted. Beverley became a major in an armoured tank division, Walter served with distinction and held officer rank in both the air force and the infantry, Robert Bramwell had a commission in the anti-tank corps. Both he and Walter saw service in New Guinea, suffered extreme malaria attacks and were wounded and hospitalised. The fourth and youngest boy, Bramwell Orams, was in the air force from the age of seventeen and flew on many sorties in the Pacific war zone. If the sisters' husbands are included there were seven men from the family in action, some in the thickest part of the New Guinea campaign. They all returned, but like so many others, they each carried scars left by the trauma of war.

Meanwhile the house in Brisbane became a household of women with even the married sisters returning for a while. Robert Burrows, now promoted to the rank of major, was in the Red Shield, acting as a welfare officer with the troops, and away from home a good deal of the time. Ella Burrows, ever the angel of mercy, organised the girls into baking tins of biscuits and cakes, and knitting a constant supply of jumpers and balaclavas for the menfolk.

It was a tense time. In London the headquarters of the Salvation Army were bombed in the blitz, and in Australia Salvation Army halls were fitted for use in an emergency. With a very real danger of invasion by Japan everybody did their bit. When Major Burrows was stationed at a camp in a nearby suburb Mrs Burrows, Eva and Margaret would take a train each Sunday afternoon to help him with the evening service he conducted for the soldiers. Eva sang and Margaret watched, filled with admiration for the sister who was only a couple of years ahead of her in age but light years away in confidence. By this time Eva was a confident happy teenager with bright shiny black eyes, straight black hair, and an attractive face with strength and life in it.

At home she belonged to the local Salvation Army corps, but gradually she became bored. Mrs Burrows didn't say 'You have to', as their father had done. Never one to miss an advantage, Eva stopped wearing uniform, vowed she would never again be seen in a bonnet and decided to do her own thing. She had had enough of Army discipline and did not share the sense of commitment she had found so attractive in her parents when she was younger. Why should the Army always come first? Or other people? What about Eva Burrows? Shouldn't she get a look in occasionally?

In many ways the rebellion was almost inevitable. Her brothers went through similar reactions with all the horrors of war to disturb their faith, and two did not stay in the Salvation Army. The teens and twenties are always a time for questioning, evaluating, making up your own mind, finding your own sense of person. Eva Burrows had a particularly forceful person with whom to come to terms. It wasn't that she went completely overboard, or examined her faith critically. She just let it lapse. There were too many other things to explore and discover.

Up to secondary school her life had revolved around the family and the Salvation Army. Now she was discovering a wider world. There was music, theatre, books. Not just the theological tomes her parents would study but whole libraries of literature and learning. She became school librarian, and always seemed to have a book in her hand. She evaded all work for studies and read incessantly. It was quite a common occurrence for one of her sisters to wake in the middle of the night and see the light burning in their father's study. They would creep in, and find Eva, fast asleep over her books.

In spite of her love of reading Eva denies being an egghead. 'I could do well, but I think how I related to people was as important as how well I did at school. I was quite keen on sports, and was in the "A" tennis and netball teams, and was the sports captain. When we went to the big competitions all the other schools in the area would be there, all the posh fee-paying schools and the church schools. We were the only state school so we were keen to do well. I would be encouraging everybody, "Come on." I suppose I had a drive to win.'

And win she did. Not only was she sports captain she was also elected head girl in her final year at school, voted there by the pupils and the staff.

'That was quite an important thing for me,' she laughs. 'To be bossing up the school. I think as far back as I can remember I was organising a group and telling people what to do.' What is more they appear to have done it, whether in small discussion groups, or the concerts and parties she helped to get under way to celebrate the ending of the war, which also came in that year.

Brisbane State High was a mixed school, and it wasn't only the girls who found Eva Burrows good company. From the time she was fourteen there was a fair amount of competition to escort this popular young lady to the cinema or school dances. Up until then the cinema had been taboo but Mrs Burrows, in her fifties and approaching retirement, was taking a broader outlook. Or perhaps she had sense to realise that in an entrenched battle she was likely to come off the worst. Margaret profited too from her sister's popularity and the relaxation in rules. Where Eva went she often followed, to outings, functions, Shakespearean plays. Eva can still remember the excitement of hearing the 'Messiah' for the first time at a concert in Brisbane. Elizabeth Schwarzkopf was another 'must' even though the ticket cost a 'phenomenal amount' to the girl whose own first public appearance had been in a best dress made from the contents of the poor box.

The Army seemed very small fry in comparison. Eva decided their activities were 'excessive', and preferred swimming or playing tennis for the school to prayer meetings. She might make a concession if it was a special occasion but otherwise she had more important things on her mind. The future, for instance. At one stage her mother had felt she would make a good doctor and did all she could to encourage her to take up medicine. Eva had a different opinion. She was becoming more and more convinced teaching should be her career. Major Burrows, back from the forces, nearly put paid to both plans. He thought Eva should leave school, and take a job, as her brothers and sisters had done. Ella Burrows dug in her heels. 'Eva is going to university if I have to go to the washtub to get her there,' she announced.

The brothers and sisters supported her. They too would have liked to have done further training. Joyce and Beverley as doctors, the brothers in other professional careers. Unfortunately there had been no money and no government assistance. Eva had excellent academic qualifications. They were all agreed. Her talents must not be wasted. Mrs Burrows won the day.

CHAPTER FIVE

Eva gained the 'magic key' to the university world when she won a government scholarship to Brisbane University at the age of seventeen. She still lived at home, handing the meagre amount of money on which she was supposed to have managed to her mother. Mrs Burrows, unknown to Eva, promptly put it in a safe place, ready for the next rung of the ladder. Eva was too busy concentrating on the first foothold to wonder what she had done with it.

In those days Salvationists were not highly educated. Captain Burrows had never had charge of a sophisticated corps. None of their friends or family had ever been to university. It was a whole new experience. Eva was apprehensive, and also she admits 'probably a bit conceited'. The first few weeks soon sorted that out. After being very much the king/queen of the castle at secondary school it was a great eye opener to find herself surrounded by all 'these brilliant and clever people'. She felt intimidated, unsure of herself. It took a while to adjust, especially to the new work patterns. At university there were fewer lectures and a large proportion of the time was supposed to be spent working on her own. Eva couldn't go home. Her father 'would have died' if one of his children had arrived home in the middle of the day, so she didn't initiate him too closely into the delights of higher education. Instead she took refuge in the library where she could read and research to her heart's content. Although she considers herself a practical, outgoing person more than an intellectual, she has always found literature a great mental enricher. She enjoyed poetry and modern novels and plays. Aldous Huxley broadened her horizons somewhat. So did meeting a wider group of friends.

During the war years everything had been circumscribed. Now she had chance to spread her wings. The social life is an important facet of university education, and Eva had always been a sociable person. She tried everything. She was still searching for the 'satisfying things in life'; somewhere she could find herself.

A Salvation Army boy who was studying medicine invited her to the Christian Union. He was a nice boy, so she went. There she discovered other young people like herself, seeking for truth and meaning. Many of them she admired, particularly the older students, and was astounded to find they were studying the Bible and not finding it boring. She began to look at it again for herself. During the vacation she went to an inter-varsity fellowship camp with a group of friends. The preacher there was Marcus Loane, who later became archbishop of all Australia, but was then only a young clergyman. He was leading Bible studies on the Book of Romans. For the first time in several years Eva found herself taking stock of her own life, realising it fell far short of the wonder and beauty of the life of Christ, and recognising she was heading in the wrong direction. Still not sure how to set things right, and with Major Burrows back from the war, she began attending the Salvation Army again.

By this time the family was based at Fortitude Valley, Brisbane, a 'tough little corps' where the larrikins had knocked down the Salvation Army lasses when they were first trying to get established, and the crowd had pelted them with mud, stones and stale fish. Like many small corps in poor areas, there had always been financial problems, but this was nothing new to Major and Mrs Burrows. They just got on with whatever task was to hand. Every year the local division (or diocese) of the Salvation Army holds special meetings for their young people, called Councils, like a war council, because so many of their terms are military. Eva and her sister Margaret, now the only ones remaining at home, went to the evening meeting. The whole of the meeting was geared to young people and the challenge of the Christian faith to them. Eva was already convinced intellectually . As the evening progressed she knew she was at a crossroads. She could go her own way, or she must hand over that rebellious will, and seek God's forgiveness for the years when she had been downright disobedient and pushed Him out of her life. She had first given her life to Him as a child, at the mercy seat in the local corps. Now she was kneeling in front of hundreds of people, weeping, making an adult decision, and so was Margaret, the timid one.

A woman knelt beside Eva, gently probing the reason for the tears. As she talked Eva revealed it was not just that she was coming back to God, but that she had realised she must give her whole self to him for the ministry. Like her parents and so many of her forbears, Eva never does anything by halves. The tears gave way to a great sense of release and peace as she and the woman prayed together. It was total commitment and the most crucial moment of her life. She readily admits she has 'always been a great enthusiast. When Christ called me . . . I gave my life, my future, everything.'

When the girls eventually reached home Major and Mrs Burrows were already in bed, but not too tired to hear the tremendous news. Margaret had not been through anything like the rebellion her sister had known, but they both shared a great sense of elation. From then on Eva was 'right in'. She knew from that moment she had to be a Salvation Army officer.

The first step was to enrol as a soldier, the Army equivalent of church membership. This involved signing the 'Articles of War' which included a statement of belief in Christ, renunciation of such evils as swearing, smoking, drinking and violence, obedience to officers and allegiance to 'carrying on the war' in which every Christian is involved. The next was to talk with a senior officer about applying as a future candidate for the ministry.

In the meanwhile there was the continuing day-to-day ministry to exercise, as young people's sergeant major in the corps, and in her studies and friendships at the university. One of Eva's aunts had a beautiful voice, and Mrs Burrows was keen for Eva to use hers. So she had singing lessons, and both Eva and Margaret learnt the art of speech and drama from a Mrs Rickwood. When plays were put on, such as Easter dramas, Eva, with her powerful voice and compelling personality, was always chosen to play the leading role. Soon the sisters were singing duets at Boothville hospital for unmarried mothers, and the local corps. The theme Eva took for her testimony at a united service in Brisbane the Good Friday after her conversion summed up her new found faith.

From my smitten heart with tears
Two wonders I confess
The wonder of His glorious love
And my own sinfulness.

To her the Cross was central. Nothing Eva Burrows could do guaranteed her salvation. Jesus had done it all. The first sermon she preached reiterated the message.

Major Burrows suffered a great deal with asthma and had taken leave from the corps for a year to try to get control of the symptoms which were becoming chronic. One Sunday morning he had a bad attack during the service. As Mrs Burrows took him from the hall she said to Eva 'You'd better finish the service'. Knowing that the sergeant-major, the most senior layman, would have been incredibly nervous Eva did as she was told. She preached about the passover, a subject they had been studying at Bible camp, and obviously made a good impression. As she shook hands with the congregation afterwards an old Salvationist thanked her and instructed, 'Always preach the blood Eva'. The little miss who had recited a 'Purple Pussycat' with such aplomb was beginning to find her true vocation. To her it was nothing out of the ordinary. She had only done what was expected of her.

'I wasn't so much bold as feeling I could accomplish things. I could do it. I would have a go.'

Margaret took a different view of the situation. She speaks of the change that took place in Eva's life at her conversion. Although she remained a strong, happy, powerful personality everything about her seemed transformed. Her growth and development was difficult to define, but it could be clearly felt by those around her. Now with years of counselling experience to her credit Margaret has more understanding of what was happening in Eva. She feels the most remarkable thing about her was her sense of 'wholeness'. She had achieved a balance between her vulnerable, nurturing, feeling side and the rational, assertive, analytical side.

At the New Year Eva and Margaret would attend holiday camps near Surfer's Paradise in the South East part of Queensland. There, Eva was always a great favourite and able to assume leadership easily. When people remarked 'Aren't you lucky to be Eva Burrows' sister', Margaret was in total agreement.

Once Eva had found her calling there was no holding her. She was so overjoyed with her Christian faith the long-term implications were of secondary importance. 'I just felt I wanted to please God,' she explains. 'Whatever it cost I would face it.'

As a soldier in the Salvation Army the cost might not have been too great. As an officer it would be much higher. Eva had seen the hard financial struggle her parents had faced. She knew the discipline required. As a single woman officer the crunch would come if she wished to marry someone who was not also an officer. She would be faced with a choice. To relinquish her calling, or the possibility of the companionship and family life which had been such an influential part of her background. She was an attractive and spirited young woman. She enjoyed the company of the opposite sex. Already at least three soldiers in her home corps had approached her father to ask about the possibility of marriage.

Eva was not interested. The young men at the university were a different matter. There were two friendships which meant a great deal to her. She dared not allow them to become too serious. She had dedicated her life totally to God. Nothing and no one could measure up to the beautiful goodness, attractive goodness she saw in its ideal perfection in Jesus Christ. Eva Burrows had found her 'shining person' and she was not going to be deflected from following Him.

CHAPTER SIX

Eva's graduation year meant more joy for the family. The day she received her BA they all had lumps in their throats and pride in their hearts. It was 'Mother's Day' particularly. Eva had the talent but Mrs Burrows had made it possible and she and Major Burrows were at Brisbane City Hall to see their daughter receive her degree. That was not the only memory they would treasure. The current General of the Salvation Army, General Orsborn, was visiting Australia. Eva had been selected as youth speaker to welcome him to Brisbane that very weekend. The General was impressed. His comments about her 'brilliant speech' were even to reach the pages of *War Cry*. Monday was graduation day. The General was holding an open air service in the square in front of City Hall. Eva, in her graduate's gown, and Major and Mrs Burrows in uniform, were amongst the crowd, planning to go straight into the ceremony after the meeting. Someone restrained them.

'Wouldn't you wait?' they requested. 'The General would like to greet you.' So there, in the forecourt , General Orsborn prayed over this new graduate recruit.

That same year, 1950, a great congress for young Salvationists from all round the world was to be held in London. It was the first event of its kind, and only possible now that traffic was beginning to move again after the restraints of the war.

Mrs Burrows was determined Eva should attend. Eva protested that they hadn't enough money. Ella silenced her arguments in one fell swoop by producing the money she had been saving from her grant all the months Eva had been at university. She might not have been able to put into words the high hopes she held for her daughter but her actions spoke volumes.

Eva took part-time work to swell the funds. In the soap factory, pineapple canning factory, anywhere she could earn quick money. Many of their Army friends subscribed towards her fare. Mrs Burrows and the sisters bought up remnants of material at the sales and 'sewed and sewed' to get Eva ready. One piece of lovely woollen material nearly defeated them. They wanted to make it into a special dress but it would not come right. At a loss about what to do next the girls stopped work. Mrs Burrows suggested taking a promise from the promise box. It read 'They that sow in tears will reap in joy.' It was sufficient for the sisters. They finished the sewing. Eva had a brand new wardrobe for only a small outlay.

There seems to have been very little resentment that Eva should have such a unique opportunity. The family were more concerned that she should 'do them proud'. They all bathed in the reflected glory of having a sister barely into her twenties who was going to travel to the other side of the world.

Not surprisingly it was Margaret who felt the parting most. She was waiting to commence training as a nurse so her life was also heading in a new direction, but she was ill prepared for the grief she was to experience at the loss of the sister who had been so close and influential in her own life.

Eva's memories are more to do with the excitement of the journey. Places such as Ceylon, Colombo, Port Said, the Suez Canal, had only been names in textbooks and beyond her wildest dreams. Now she was on board RMS *'Otranto'* watching the place names spring to life. With her were thirty nine other young Australian Salvationists. They included an engineer, a nurse, three accountants, a laboratory assistant and a secretary. They travelled cheaply. In 1950 the journey cost £65 sterling, and took six weeks. There were six to a cabin and they were on deck H. The initial was appropriate. At times the heat could become unbearable so they slept on deck as they came through the Suez Canal.

In true Salvation Army style the six weeks were not wasted. There were Bible studies on deck four afternoons each week, special meetings for the children on board, and timbrel practice at 7.45am. On the final evening almost two hundred people gathered for an informal service in which young people's sergeant major Eva Burrows was one of the leaders. As the meeting closed the ship's engines stopped. The excited delegates ran to the rail. There in the distance were the lights of London.

It took until the afternoon of the next day for everyone to disembark, and the boat train to deposit its excited passengers at St Pancras station. A fast trip through central London whisked them past the main tourist attractions and out to the suburbs to the International Training College where they were to stay. A hurried tea and they were on the move again. Someone had told them there was to be a memorial service for Evangeline Booth that evening in the Regent Hall, which had once been a skating rink. They decided they had to go.

'You get on the bus to the Elephant and Castle,' an innocent Londoner informed them. 'Then you get the underground to Oxford Circus.'

The Australians looked at one another. Elephants? Circuses? In the middle of a city? What was this London they were being set loose in? By the time they found out they were late. The only remaining seats were at the front. They tried to creep in surreptitiously during the singing of the first song. Above them, on the platform, stood the General and a whole row of Commissioners, the territorial leaders of the Army. Eva and her companions were amazed. Back home you only ever saw one at a time.

The meeting concluded with a final song of praise for the life of Evangeline Booth and her striking leadership.

Springing to his feet one of the Australian contingent took the flag and led the group, clapping and singing, in a 'Glory march' round the hall. With a certain amount of understatement the Army missionary magazine *All the World* reported, 'It was one of the most remarkable memorial services ever witnessed in the old "Rink".' The Salvation Army in the Western world had grown a certain veneer of sophistication. They were not used to all this fervour and zeal. Neither were they over familiar with the tambourine. Timbrel groups were almost unknown in Great Britain, and the few instruments around were certainly not played with the vigour and movement familiar to the Australians. When the Australian girls performed in the Royal Albert Hall arms swirling, ribbons flying, everyone went wild. The folk from down under were certainly making their presence felt. Photographs of the Congress show Indian girls in their saris and young men and women from all round the world, Jamaica, Ceylon, Japan, South America. There are few more striking than the slim sergeant major with the dark eyes, pronounced eyebrows and nose, and dark hair rolled at the nape of her neck. Though not yet an officer, she was leading the Australian delegation and the timbrel group, 'an outstanding young woman even in those days'.

With over a thousand delegates from thirty three countries to choose from her impact must have been pretty powerful. So was the Congress. It brought together on a grand scale the children of many nations whose parents and older brothers would have fought on opposing sides in the war. For most it would have been their first experience of the internationalism of the movement. There were Bible studies and discussions, debate about the future of the Salvation Army, trips round the East End of London where the Founder had walked, a visit to the bombed International Headquarters, and spectacular events like a big march through London down Whitehall to Hyde Park. Many of the delegates were later to become officers, and although Eva did not realise it at the time people in high places were again taking note of her presence. As she committed her life once more to God's service at the conclusion of one of the big meetings an old retired officer who had been specially invited knelt next to her at the mercy seat. He was Commissioner Allister Smith, a pioneer of the work amongst the Zulus, and famous in Salvation Army missionary history. General Orsborn recognised both him and the young Australian who had given him such a memorable welcome to her homeland.

'Here is a young person,' he remarked. 'And an old saint of God. There's always room at the place of prayer for the young and old.'

CHAPTER SEVEN

After all the excitement of a major event a time of exhaustion and deflation tends to set in when it is over. In Eva's case another surprise was in store. She had planned to work for a year in England then take a post-graduate certificate in education at London University before going home to do her officer training in Australia. The principal of the William Booth Memorial College in Denmark Hill, which had been opened by Bramwell the year before Eva's birth, had other ideas. He too was Australian and had watched Eva's progress since she was a small girl.

'Why don't you come and do your theological training now before you go to university?' he suggested.

Eva was taken aback. In those days it was unusual for an Australian to train in Britain. Her parents were expecting her to go to the college they themselves had attended. On the other hand, it made sense. She knew it was right to go to London University because she hoped one day to teach in Africa, and they had a special course in education in relation to tropical areas. It would simply mean missing out the year teaching. Eva prayed, and made her decision. She cabled her parents and told them she was going to the Salvation Army College in London.

Eva was twenty one that September. Major and Mrs Burrows knew she was more than capable of weighing up the pros and cons, and living with the consequences. They accepted her judgement. Beverley was a tougher nut to crack. He had become a major in the military at twenty four and achieved much in the world in prosperity and position, but it had been an uphill climb. Now here was this gifted sister, who had so many opportunities that he had been denied, apparently threatening to throw them all down the drain, and bury herself in some backwater in Africa. Eventually, as in most family crises, the initial shock wore off, and everyone simmered down. All their lives the Burrows children had been trained to 'Give God the glory'. Wasn't Eva doing just that? They must support her all they could.

She was going to need that support. Training for officership meant that her physical needs were provided for, but there was no pay. Eva already had the uniforms she had brought with her for the youth congress. She only needed a few more bits and pieces. Then she must conserve the small amount of money remaining. There had never been much spare cash in the Burrows household. Living economically almost came as second nature. It did not take the family long to appreciate her situation. Gifts from them helped eke out her limited income throughout her training and over the next several years.

That autumn saw Eva standing on the steps of the dark brick building in Denmark Hill, with its high surrounding wall, and predominant tower. A training officer of that era described the college not as 'an educational seminary, but a spiritual power house'. The nine-month period of apprenticeship included Bible study, history and doctrine of the Salvation Army, and lessons in finance, organisation and preaching, with the emphasis on the heart as much as the head. The qualities the leaders were looking for were 'faith and character that will stand the test of hardwork, frugal living, discipline and responsibility.' The students were expected to spend half an hour at the beginning of each day in quiet study and prayer, and there were private interviews with the tutors about the candidates spiritual life, growth and development.

'You accepted the fact that you were there to be developed, improved and polished,' Eva comments, even if in her case she once took it rather too literally.

The day began at 6.30 am when beds had to be made and rooms tidied. Then the students took turns doing such duties as waiting at table, washing up and cleaning the college steps. One Friday morning the sergeant in charge of Eva's brigade gave her the task of cleaning the brass window winders and door handles in the assembly hall. Eva polished away with a will, thinking of Samuel in the temple who did even the most menial work for God. Her enthusiasm was short lived. That afternoon in free time the sergeant stopped her, and told her the work hadn't been done properly. Distressed, Eva hurried inside. What had she failed to do? On the floor beneath the handles was a series of white blobs where the cleaner had dripped. Now she had to clean the floor as well.

'I think I learnt a few things,' laughs Eva though at the time it must have been extremely painful for the girl who had 'excelled at everything'.

Part of the course involved criticism of the cadets' sermons and talks. Eva was back in her natural environment. She had inherited her mother's gift of speaking simply and directly, yet still being challenging and thought provoking. Her problems were more to do with the self confidence which had characterised her from such an early age. The reserved British could quickly interpret it as brashness. She readily admits 'Many people thought I was a bit forward. I would just go up and speak to anybody, including the leaders, as if they were equals. I suddenly discovered I was very much down the bottom of the pile.'

There were times when she must have been something of a pain to her superiors, but once again people were beginning to take note of her talents. In fact it would have been difficult not to notice Eva Burrows. For a start she was a graduate, and although intellectual ability was by no means the main criterion she took her studies seriously and came top of the class in most subjects. She had a beautiful singing voice, played the tambourine in an unusual way, had a 'nice uniform cape in a style no one had ever seen before', and an accent that drew immediate attention.

Added to all this she was interested in people. With two hundred students it was impossible for her to know everyone but she enjoyed the air of camaraderie, companionship, being in it together, the sense of fun. Two of Eva's closest friends date from that time – Ingrid Lindberg who is now head of the Salvation Army in Finland, and Miriam Vinti, who is a leader in her home territory, Italy.

Approximately ten of the students came from outside Britain, and Eva took a special interest in them. They had lots in common, including separation from their families. Eva has never been one to indulge in self pity but she must have missed the warmth of the Australian sun, and the family back home. When the students had free time she used to like to go down to Camberwell to a flower seller who sold mimosa, which is a kind of wattle. No matter how she might have to count the pennies she could always spare a few for the bright yellow flowers which reminded her of home.

Fraternising with the boys was not encouraged. Strict separation was the order of the day, forcing some couples to leave notes in drainpipes and resort to all kinds of strategies if they wished to communicate more than a passing word. William Booth had once instructed that if anyone notified Headquarters of an intended engagement they should 'Put a few hundred miles between them. That'll show whether or not they're in earnest', and his strictures were taken seriously. Nevertheless several girls did meet their future husbands during the course. Why not the lively lass from down under?

For one thing, the war was only a matter of a few years in the past and the number of potential suitors must have been severely limited, especially of the right intellect and calibre. There were those who were interested and showed their interest in the following year but by that time officership was foremost in Eva's thoughts. 'I was very much dedicated to the purpose God had for me. Possibly some of the men might have been a bit intimidated. I think even then I saw that the single life, the celibate life, was to be part of God's plan, and I didn't rebel against it. I think all along the line I felt a great sense of privilege at being able to share the gospel, and that God had chosen, and was going to use me. That might sound naive to some people but to me it was like a flowering of my life. The beauty of the flower was for God.'

Evangelism has always been the order of the day in the training and strategies of the Salvation Army, as its name implies. Eva's desire to communicate the gospel was given plenty of outlets. Her apprenticeship included door-to-door visitation, 'Pub booming' and taking part in both indoor and open air meetings. Eva's voice lessons were to be put to good effect. Every week they were out on the streets of Highgate or Chalk Farm preaching, and Eva belonged to the cadet's singing brigade. One day Eva and Ingrid were selling *War Cry* in a pub in London when a rowdy crowd asked them to sing 'The Old Rugged Cross,' a favourite hymn in the 1940s and 1950s. Hastily improvising they did as they were asked.

The chilly wind of February brought the annual self-denial appeal. Finance has always been a headache for a group whose adherents have often come from amongst the poorest strata of society. Officers themselves receive an 'allowance' little above subsistence level. One enthusiastic supporter more than a century ago offered to go without pudding for a year to raise much-needed funds. This 'touched Booth more deeply than any lavish endowment' but he was loathe for his officer to deny himself for such a long stretch of time. In the end they compromised. A week of self giving should not be too much for anyone. The idea caught on. That year alone self-denial week raised nearly five thousand pounds. It became an annual event and a major source of Army income, with the public soon being asked to share in the exercise.

Eva and several of the cadets from overseas were put in the West End brigade to do their bit. They had to stand practically from morning to night outside the big department stores and theatres with heavy collecting boxes, asking for donations. As usual Eva entered into the spirit of the thing with energy and determination. By the end of the week she had done very well with her collecting and made several interesting contacts.

The nine months flew by. Enough material was packed into the curriculum to last two or three years. By May the cadets had come to the end of their training. The aim of the college was 'To produce a man and woman whom no emergency will find wanting.' It was nearly as tall an order as Eva's father had set before her at the beginning of her life. The cadets seemed undaunted. They were going out into the world though none of them knew quite where until it was announced in public at their Commissioning Service in the Albert Hall. Eva discovered she was to go to Portsmouth, a naval port on the south coast, until she started her studies at London University. Sometimes there were tears, sometimes great excitment at the appointments. Eva took it all in her stride. In her eyes it was only a stepping stone. Her sights were set on Africa and the wider horizons she hoped would be possible after her tropical studies. The only regret was that her parents could not come to England for her commissioning, though a report in the Australian *War Cry* announced that she had come 'Dux' of the session and had trained the women cadets for the timbrel play at the commissioning.

Ingrid, her close friend and companion, knew that was only the outward achievment. What had really counted to Eva was the covenant service preceding the commissioning. There the cadets made their promises and signed a covenant form binding themselves to the service of God and the Salvation Army 'all their days'. Eva meant every word. 'Her sincerity in wanting to serve the Lord was unmistakable. She entered her life's work full of joy at being allowed to give herself wholly to the Lord's service.'

CHAPTER EIGHT

Portsmouth presented a unique opportunity for putting the theory of the training college into practice. Newly commissioned cadets are normally sent to work in a relatively small situation. Portsmouth was a large corps. The officers were two single ladies, and one had been unwell. Eva was sent in as support. From the word go she was knocking on doors, visiting and sharing the platform ministry every Sunday. 'It was a very good training. The officer, Major Lilian Glase, was the walking epitome of what a Salvation Army officer should be.'

By October she was back in London, billeted in a students' hostel at Southampton Row, and worshipping at Regent Hall, where the Australian group had made such an impact the night of their arrival in Britain for the International Youth Congress. She became a member of the Salvation Army Students' Fellowship and was soon fully involved in university life.

Her fellow students at the Institute of Education in Mallen Street were preparing for work in many different parts of the world; Africa, India, Cyprus. Everybody had to do a mini thesis and Eva chose the presentation of the gospel in the Third World. She was encouraged to study education, anthropology and African religion besides 'doing a little about missions in the Third World'. Some of the students were African and her tutor, Mrs Baggott, had worked as a missionary in Nigeria. She gave Eva plenty of scope to prepare her mind for the whole matter of the interpretation of the gospel in Africa, and how to make the good news relevant in a non-Christian environment.

It was a very helpful preparation and gave her a first real taste of teaching. Her practice school was a secondary school near Roman Road market in London's East End, birthplace of the Salvation Army and famous for pie and mash, West Ham football club and the current television soap opera *Eastenders*. Teaching history and religious education to cockney teenagers must have been something of a culture shock, but Eva seems to have thrived on it, and the lively East End lads would have appreciated her outgoing personality and no nonsense approach. She didn't wear Salvation Army uniform in school, but she used to visit a Goodwill centre in Bethnal Green and nothing of note escapes the eager eyed cockney. When she asked her pupils the name of one of the disciples quick as a flash came the answer, 'Matthew . . . cap'n.'

The end of the academic year came round almost as speedily. It was time for farewell to England and a brief return to Australia for a much-needed holiday. The boat trip should have provided some respite but it is difficult to see how. Part of Booth's schemes to improve the lot of the disadvantaged in society had included plans for an overseas colony. During his lifetime the suggestion was treated with hostility in Australia but migration schemes were under way by the 1920s. When she set sail for her homeland in 1952 Eva and another Australian girl were given the job of looking after twelve children from the Fairbridge Society on the voyage. There were ten boys and two girls, ranging from six to fourteen years, going to start a new life on the farm schools in Australia. It was quite an experience. The purser gave them part of the ship where they could do 'all sorts of things in the morning – singing, drawing, competitions'. It wasn't long before other families on board were sending their children to join in the fun.

The few weeks with her own family flew past. By October Eva was being farewelled from Australia to 'her first appointment on missionary service to the Howard Institute in Southern Rhodesia' (Australian *War Cry* November 15th 1952). At the service she prayed that God would fill her heart with love for the people to whom she was to minister. Like mothers the world over Mrs Burrows must have watched and pondered, and wondered just what God's plan for her offspring would be, but she never expressed any doubts. Eva said, 'When I went to Africa she never mentioned once that I shouldn't go. She was always very positive. She felt if that was my desire and what God wanted she was happy to stand by me. But I believe she always felt that I had leadership potential and that one day I would have great responsibility.'

Even though a state of emergency was declared in Kenya that same month none of the family seemed particularly perturbed. Eva was doing the Lord's will and the Lord would look after her. Salvation Army missionary history included illness and tragedy, but it also had its success stories like Howard Institute where Eva was heading. It had been established nearly thirty years in the Chiweshe reserve, an area of land for African development, fifty miles north of the capital city, Salisbury. The quality of the land varied but was mainly second class. Soil erosion was not helped by the over-stocking of cattle which were regarded as wealth, and essential for paying 'lobola' or bride-price. The main crop was maize, and harvests varied with the weather and farming methods. In a bad year the crops could fail completely. The people were poor. The only ones with a steady income were teachers, storekeepers and local officials. Many of the males went to work in town and sent back a little money occasionally. Home was a round hut, or rondavel, with mud walls and a grass roof.

It was a picturesque area ringed with kopjes, wooded hills with great rocks protruding from them. Elephants and lions roamed the uncultivated areas. Water was comparatively plentiful, except in times of drought, but the pools and streams were infested with the parasites which caused bilharzia, a debilitating disease which infected nearly all the local people, who had no alternative water supply for washing. Malnutrition, malaria and various worms added to the health problems.

Although other Christian groups such as the Methodists and Catholics were active in Rhodesia a kind of gentleman's agreement meant each kept within a fairly well defined territory. The Chiweshe reserve was almost entirely dependent on the Salvation Army for Christian worship, education and health care. There were twenty or more Salvation Army centres, and most had their own church and school. Each year the Salvation Army held a congress in Chiweshe where twenty thousand Salvationists would meet. The march of uniformed members took more than an hour to pass the saluting base.

Howard was regarded as a working fulfilment of the three-fold commission to teach, preach the gospel and heal the sick. There was a farm and plantation of a hundred acres and a hospital with fifty beds for in-patients, plus outpatient facilities. The education work included a village primary school with five hundred pupils, a central primary school equivalent to what would now be counted as secondary education, a teacher training school with fifty students and a Salvation Army officer's Training College. The central feature was the Salvation Army Hall where each Sunday a march by most of the senior students with flags flying and drums beating would be followed by worship. At any given time during term there could be up to a thousand people on the compound.

Many of these facts would have been known to Eva as she took the four-day journey by train from Cape Town to land-locked Rhodesia. What she didn't know was quite what life on a mission station would be like or how she would adjust to it, though it doesn't appear to have given her any sleepless nights. In true Burrows' fashion she was looking forward to it and convinced that this was what God wanted her to do. The officer delegated to collect her from the station seems to have been more disconcerted than she was . His stereotyped image of the single missionary lady was overturned with one stupendous 'Wow' once he had met the outgoing Australian with the warm smile and alert interest in everything around her. Typically it wasn't the buildings, or the country, that first impressed Eva. It was the people. 'I just remember feeling at home. I never had a sense of being disorientated in Africa.'

The overseas personnel at Howard came from many different countries; America, Canada, Norway, New Zealand, Denmark, Britain. Eva shared a delapidated house with an American girl, Helen Rosser. The walls were unbaked bricks, the roof corrugated sheets. It was small and very old. At first she was a bit shocked by the primitive conditions. The roads were unmade, the water supply erratic though the constant sunshine from February to November compensated for a lot of things. Because they were five thousand feet above sea level the climate was marvellous, apart from the wet season. Then ants would crawl through the cracks in the floor and build a big nest in the middle of the bedroom. To add insult to injury the roof leaked. It was just too much for the American girl when they were faced one day with yet another torrential downpour.

'Just think of Dr Livingstone,' chided Eva, who knew he had travelled through that area. 'He didn't even have a roof over his head.'

'What makes you think we have?' growled her companion, unimpressed.

CHAPTER NINE

One of the first tasks Eva set herself was learning the local language, Shona. She loved to walk out into the villages where she would sit round the fire or outside a hut shelling peanuts with a family, so that she learned first hand many of the African customs and quickly mastered the language. Soon she was fluent in conversation and public speaking though as a young lieutenant she felt very much a beginner.

'I didn't see myself as bossing the Africans. I never had that white supremacy idea, and I don't think I was paternalistic. I felt I was learning so much. I made a lot of mistakes as any young person does, but I never made the mistake of thinking I knew it all as far as the Africans were concerned.'

When she walked into a village the Africans would often clap their hands in a reverential way. She would acknowledge their greeting then the language would 'flow from her' and their eyes would light up in response. It was a relationship of mutual respect. She was eager to know about the people; their language, background, culture, history. They welcomed the extrovert young Australian who was so genuine in her concern for their children and spoke their language with far more than her lips.

Her teaching career began in the Central Primary School. There were few secondary schools in Rhodesia in the early 1950s so there was fierce competition for places. Out of seventy children in the village school only sixteen could go on to further education after the age of ten or eleven. In a letter home to Australia Eva described the sombre silence, concentrated look and earnestness of purpose shown by her students at examination time. She knew the value, and cost, of education from her own family's sacrifices and empathised with the country's desperate need for more teachers and schools. In the meantime she could only help them as best she could which, being Eva Burrows, was a great deal.

She had a natural gift for teaching and was rated 'an excellent member of staff, capable and enthusiastic,' with boundless energy and very much in command in any situation. She loved organising things and being with young people, whether it was debating society, Saturday night socials, musical activities, sports, whatever. She would join in anything. It was a familiar sight to see her running up and down the sideline refereeing, or getting out her bike to cycle out to the reserve to organise Guides. Ingrid, who joined her at Howard a couple of years after leaving college, got hauled in to help with Brownies and go camping in grass shelters the girls had built. Whether sleeping under the starry African sky with wild animals roaming in the bush was part of the fun or genuine cause for concern it did not seem to disturb Eva who was always fast asleep as soon as her head touched the pillow.

Many of the pupils were boarders so part of the duties included supervising the compound where the students lived. Saturday morning was set aside for cleaning and general tidying up. Roads had to be swept, grass and flowers trimmed. There were classrooms to be cleaned, dormitories, the hall, the church. By the end of Saturday morning the whole place was spick and span, with hopefully not too many drops of cleaner on the floor when it came to inspection time. In the afternoon the pupils could relax playing games though the staff still had to be on their toes refereeing. Saturday evening meant social activities – films, discussions, general celebration. Each night the teachers had to take turns checking that the students were in their dormitories, and the lights were out at an appropriate time. Eva would often pause on her evening rounds to sit with the girls and share their fun or more serious discussions. 'She was a very popular teacher because of her personal interest in them. She got to know so much about the individual and her home circumstances.'

Within two years she had been transferred from teaching to teacher training. Initially she taught academic subjects: maths, English, geography. Before long she was involved in the more professional areas; methods of teaching, principles, organisation of schools, the supervision of teaching practice. Much of this was new to Eva and Ingrid, who now shared a house with her, as well as the work at the teacher training college, and they spent many late nights in preparation.

It was a long day. School started at 7am, and went through to four in the afternoon with a break at lunchtime. After school there would be games, Guides, all kinds of activities, and a couple of hours homework to supervise. On top of that there could be time spent tutoring individual pupils with special needs before they had time to think of preparation for the next day. It was perhaps just as well Eva was a sound sleeper, who could manage on five or six hours sleep, and be up before breakfast doing language study.

She faced it all with cheerful enthusiasm. Her aim was to produce not just good teachers but good Christian teachers, with a concern for their country and its future.She knew from her own experience that the whole person needed to be developed, not just a robot only capable of regurgitating examination fodder. Her Bible talks to the students were always practical and direct.

'I think I created around me always a positive sense of what you can become. Jesus had great faith in people. He would bring out the best. A lot of our joy came from the growth and development of our students.'

Education was not just a bait to hook souls. The staff at Howard were intent on giving their students the best they could offer. At that time almost 90% of the whole education programme of Rhodesia was in the hands of missionaries and there was a great and growing demand. Throughout those years there was a constant building and re-building programme at Howard. The emphasis of the training was always on the practical side, helping the students to do things for themselves, and not to rely too heavily on imported materials. Students would go out from college with great boxes of equipment which had been made very simply and inexpensively, using local, natural materials wherever possible.

End of term was always a tense time, when the inspectors from the African Education Department came out from Salisbury to assess the students' teaching ability. One inspector was particularly strict and everybody dreaded his visit but Eva could do no wrong in his eyes. She got the results. In fact the success rate at Howard was so high it was once queried and re-checked.

Eva was less surprised. She knew only the cream would have been able to get to Teacher Training College in the first place, and so many shared her desire and enthusiasm for education. Besides, there was the sacrifice their parents had made to send them to school. Education everywhere in Africa was fee paying and when students came to Howard they all had to pay boarding fees. Eva knew from her conversations with the villagers the high hopes that parents had for their children. Failure would be such a terrible thing. How could she fail them?

The parents' sacrifice wasn't the only one. The teachers at Howard were given government grants for their work but the money they received was the standard Salvation Army allowance. Any excess earning, maybe 50-60% of their wages, would be ploughed into Howard Institute. On one occasion Eva visited Bulawayo where she met people working for other organisations. They had their own flats, a car, were able to live comfortably. Eva reported it all as a matter of fact. There was no sense of grievance. She just accepted the way things were done in the Army.

She also did her bit to encourage those in a much tighter situation than her own. One of her students, Simon, was having difficulty gathering the money to pay his yearly fees, despite working every available holiday. When she received a gift from the Queensland corps back in Australia she used it to help Simon. If something needed doing Eva Burrows didn't look around for someone else to see to it. She just got on and did it. 'If people said "Oh no – I don't want to do that" I used to be so surprised.'

So how did she feel about becoming corps officer? A task which involved organising all the Sunday services, Sunday school and several weeknight activities. Wasn't she entitled to some time of her own after a busy week's teaching and little free time on Saturday? The idea probably never entered her head.

Officers took turns in conducting the Sunday morning service but every Sunday evening Eva would be up the front conducting the soldiers' meeting. Students and staff were encouraged to take part but Eva would lead the songs and choruses with her clear voice, making sure that 'adequate time and attention was given to prayer and thorough instruction as to what was required of a Salvation Army soldier'. The meetings were never dull. Eva could enter into the exuberance and singing of African life wholeheartedly and Sunday evenings were no exception. Drums are basic to African rhythm and beat. It only took a little adaptation for many familiar songs to take on a new life and vigour, especially with the accompaniment of timbrels, clapping and dancing. 'In Salvation Army meetings Africans do jump around and dance quite a bit.'

So does Eva Burrows. When African music is part of a meeting her staff speculate about how long she will be able to keep still. African tribal beliefs gave her more serious pause for thought. She had too great a respect for the people to discount their inherited wisdom and instinctive worship of a power beyond themselves. From her studies and the things people had shared she felt there were strong links between the Christian faith and the Bantu religious background.

'In that part of Africa there was a belief in one God, Mwari, but he was great and far away. You came to him through the spirits of your ancestors so that spirit worship and fear of the spirits of your relatives was very real to the people.'

Westerners might dismiss spirit possession as auto-suggestion or the effects of worms and other debilitating diseases, but the effect on those who believed in its power could not be disputed. Although Eva was a bystander on more than one occasion when dramatic and scary incidents occurred such matters were generally dealt with by the African officers who understood the cultural background and could use language and symbolism the people would understand in order to 'exorcise' the spirit.

Communication is one of the key words in Eva's own approach to people and in her understanding of Christianity. She saw Jesus Christ as the bridge between God and man, who showed just how much God loves us and gave access to Him without the need of other intermediaries. She felt he was the culmination of the African's search rather than in conflict. It was not a glib doctrinal position simply culled from the inherited opinions of her own Christian forbears, but the result of many years study and patient listening to all that the African students and officers could teach. In return her own deep awareness of God and feeling for Him communicated on a much deeper level than mere words. She could talk in quite rough and ready language if occasion demanded. She was not pious. Her religion was part of life, just as the Africans was. They prayed before they planted their seeds. They prayed before they cooked their food. When they saw the mission folk were as sincere in their beliefs they were happy to accept and join in.

'The sad thing is so many of them thought every white person is a Christian and of course they're not, and a lot of them became disillusioned and wide open to communism,' said Eva.

Eva's positive faith and vibrant personality struck many chords. By the end of her first term in office the Australian *War Cry* was reporting that all but one of the forty nine students at the training college had passed their final exam and that twenty eight of the first year students had become Salvationists and eight had applied to be officers.

It would not have been surprising if Eva's many gifts and accomplishments had brought the temptation to pride. Certainly she could be rebellious at times in her nature but she was always quick to re-dedicate herself to what she felt to be God's will. An officer who worked alongside her for many years interpreted the fact that he had seen her kneeling at the mercy seat more than any other officer as a sign of her close relationship with God and the constant need for the kind of realignment which requires a certain humbling of oneself. Eva is less certain. She feels her Australian temperament has left her with fewer inhibitions than her European counterparts.

Whatever her spiritual battles her sense of humour has to be a saving grace , especially when she is not afraid to laugh at herself. The lessons in singing and elocution had left her with a pretty powerful voice. Too powerful for the technicians at the local radio station. An octet from Howard was invited to sing for some religious programmes. While the rest of the group stood around the microphone Eva was invited to move over to the corner. 'It wasn't that I had a louder voice. Just more resonant. More penetrating.'

However much teasing that must have provoked, her voice has been a considerable advantage over the years. Maybe never more so than when she accompanied a group of cadets training for officership on a ten-day campaign in remote rural areas. They held a big meeting near a mine compound one evening and hundreds of people had gathered to listen. It was very dark and several of the men were drunk. The crowd became noisy and restless. The cadets apprehensive. Eva was asked to sing. Unaccompanied she began to sing in the local language. A hush fell over the crowd and the meeting continued unhindered.

Eva related a similar incident some thirty years later at a meeting entitled 'Give to Jesus Glory'. In the story she recalled it was slides of the life of Christ which had stilled the crowd. She hadn't even remembered her own contribution until someone reminded her afterwards.

CHAPTER TEN

In spite of the long hours and sense of being almost constantly on call it wasn't all work at Howard. Some of the officers had gramophones and records and it was in Africa that Eva really got to love classical music. There were few opportunities for attending concerts but passers-by became used to the familiar sound of Mozart's 'Jupiter' symphony or Handel's water music floating from Eva's house in the lunchtime break. If she wanted something less serious the musical show 'My Fair Lady' was a regular choice. The song 'Why can't a woman be more like a man?' was a special favourite, appealing to her sense of fun.

Radio brought the main news from the outside world; nuclear tests in the Pacific, civil rights marches in America, the coronation of Queen Elizabeth and the 'never had it so good' era in Britain. *Time* magazine was another way of keeping up with Western life. Eva read it from cover to cover; films, music, book reviews as well as the politics. Books came from the central library in Salisbury by the train load.

When that was too much like work there were all the domestic tasks to catch up on. Eva had good taste in the home. She liked bold colours. Van Gogh's 'Sunflowers' dominated her living room along with a painting by a famous aboriginal artist. Much of the routine work was done by girl students eager to earn a little extra towards their fees. At first this seemed strange to some of the staff who saw it as only one step away from slavery. The girls regarded it in a different light. To them it was much needed money and a chance to learn extra skills in cooking or housekeeping. Eva herself was a good cook and often made cakes on a Saturday morning which 'she presented with pride and joy'.

Her garden was another delight. She would dig and cultivate her plants with great gusto and had one of the finest gardens in the Institute compound. The results would be used to decorate the house or hall where her artistic flair again showed in the colour and composition of her arrangements. When there were no flowers in the garden she would pick seed pods and wild things from the forest. The daughter of a Norwegian couple, Elizabeth, would often accompany her, and was obviously taking note.

One day at home when mother was arranging flowers Elizabeth informed her 'Mummy, you're not doing it right. You shouldn't be using scissors.'

'Of course you should,' her mother replied indignantly. 'It's right.'

'No, it isn't,' Elizabeth insisted. 'Auntie Eve cuts them with her teeth.'

When it came to dressmaking the boot was on the other foot. Some of the staff were domestic science teachers and Eva was eager to listen to the advice of her colleagues and put into practice anything new she learned. None of the officers had much money to spare so practically all their clothes were hand made, including their uniforms. Short sleeved dresses were the order during the working week, but they also made proper long sleeved uniforms with stand up collars and all the buttons and trimmings. Memories of the marathon 'sew-in' before she left home for the International Youth Congress could not have failed to bring a smile to Eva's lips, or those of her sisters , if they could have seen her stitching away patiently and efficiently on a hand-driven sewing machine.

Being a sociable person Eva loved entertaining. She would set the table with the best glass and cutlery she could lay her hands on, and her meals always had something a little different about them. Maybe the conversation had something to do with it, for Eva had no intention of letting her interests deteriorate however far out in the bush they might be, and she was rarely at loss for an anecdote or conversation starter. Whenever there were parties , which were a fairly regular occurrence with twenty five staff and no other form of entertainment, Eva Burrows was always 'the centre of happenings'. She was so full of life. Off duty she would 'leave her dignity behind, sing and tell stories until everybody had a good time'.

In the quieter moments Scrabble might be the order of the day. Not just one game , but two or three in a row, with Eva more often than not the winner. It seemed she could enjoy herself whatever she was doing, but she had to be doing something. Tennis, walking, dancing with the older women she met in the villages. She was always on the move. The children of the other missionaries loved her. 'Auntie Eve' could always be relied on to take an interest in their studies, or come up with something exciting such as a picnic or a day in the bush when they were home from boarding school. She even made a miniature Guide uniform for one four-year-old tot, and popped her on the back of her bicycle when she went out to the reserve for Guide meetings.

A slightly older child was given the task of colouring in a picture for part of her correspondence lessons. When her mother came into the room the picture was completed but the grass had all been coloured blue. Mother remonstrated, but the child had her reasons. 'Auntie Eve loves Blue Grass.'

Belonging to such a close community helped assuage some of the loneliness Eva could have felt so far from her own close-knit family. With most people homesickness was inevitable but Eva had already been away from her family for several years and had never been a person to sit and pine for long. There was too much to do. She never missed writing to her parents though, and the family made sure she had a regular supply of correspondence and gifts.

Dorothy and her husband worked tirelessly for the various mission projects.

'They filled their mission tins over and over with money they collected from selling fruit and vegetables from their garden, eggs from their hens, and jams and preserves made from their own grapes and citrus fruit.'

People were most conscious of how far they were from their family in times of crisis, when someone was sick or dying and they were a couple of continents away separated by a long slow haul by boat and train. For the married couples the heartache would be centred round their children going off to boarding school, especially when they left home for the first time. Then they needed the special consolation or encouragement of the substitute family at Howard; the camaraderie of the other single girls, or the understanding of families who had shared the same kind of sadness. Many of the staff found that their closest friends still date from that era.

'There was a great deal of affection amongst us. Now when we meet the years roll away. Like with your own family.' There had to be when they were working together, worshipping, tripping over one another in their free time, perhaps even sharing a house.

That is not to say there were no clashes of temperament or differences of opinion about the way things should be done. Howard attracted many gifted people who have subsequently attained leadership roles in the Salvation Army. Their keen intellects and powerful personalities could spark off more than just brilliant ideas at times. Eva herself had a 'natural sense of leadership but fitted very well into the staff team and was content to serve to the utmost of her powers as she was directed by her leaders'. She also had strong opinions and found it hard to 'brook any delay or frustration. If she'd set her mind on something she thought was right she would want it done immediately. Or five minutes before'.

If somebody failed to come up to her own high standards the directness she had inherited from her Australian background meant they would soon know. Those of a similar calibre gave as good as they got. The sensitive souls found her more difficult to stomach. She had so many talents. She had a warm, affectionate nature, but she was a professional in all she did; her work, worship, relaxation, appearance, home. How could lesser mortals fail to feel inadequate in comparison?

'She was a person you couldn't be neutral about. You either liked her very much, or you didn't.'

Her identification with the Africans could be another source of tension. An older woman officer made it her business to tell her when she had done wrong, and she admits to at least one incident she seriously mishandled. Her eyes deepen at the memory. It is an obvious cause for grief. That same ability to identify helps her appreciate the hurts she may sometimes have caused others. She is no plaster saint. She acknowledges her faults and is quick to ask forgiveness when she knows she has overstepped the line.

The principal of Howard, Colonel Rive, was a very wise leader, whom many of the staff regarded almost as a father figure. His first wife, who later died of cancer, was also a reconciling person. 'If two people had some disagreement she could find a way of softening that situation. I think we all saw that strained relationships amongst the staff greatly affect the students. So we tended to subordinate any feelings of anger for the wellbeing of the whole community. We took each other with all our faults. Much the same as in a family.'

The staff 'spiritual' meetings on Friday night and the ever-present mercy seat also helped to ensure no grievance simmered on for too long, though 'it wasn't an angelic community by any means'. Which is hardly surprising given fallible human nature.

With only one lorry and one car to supply all the needs of the two dozen overseas staff there was no way to escape other people or one's own negative traits which could become glaringly obvious living in such confined quarters.

September to October, 'the suicide months', posed a special hazard as the heat and humidity built up in preparation for the rainy season. A sudden storm or hiccup in the generator which supplied electricity could plunge the whole compound into darkness. An even worse calamity occurred when the bore hole pump packed up. Over one thousand people had no water.

It was a simple frugal life. The African staple diet was a solid, stodgy porridge, called sazda, made from pounded maize supplemented with vegetables and a little meat, when any was available. The missionary officers had their groceries delivered twice a week by lorry from the nearest store which was nine or ten miles away. They grew their own vegetables, much to the delight of the villagers' cows, who enjoyed a free dinner on more than one occasion. 'Mealies', or corn on the cob, and the occasional scrawny chicken could be bought in the village. Fruit grew on the compound: a few bananas, lemons, mangoes, pawpaw and avacado pears weighing up to a pound and a half.

In the rainy season roads became a quagmire, irrespective of who was going to travel them, including the Governor General. When the staff knew he was coming to visit the school the whole place was spring cleaned. It was a long straight drive from the main gates up to the entrance of the compound, and the stones which marked the main track had all been specially whitened. During the night there was torrential rain. The students and staff were up at 5am re-painting the stones and filling up the holes in the road. What they failed to realise was that the rain had washed the topsoil down the slope and banked it up behind the gate so that when the Governor General and his entourage arrived nobody could open the gate.

'All sorts of funny things could happen. You always had to be prepared for anything.'

Looking back the staff who worked there are amazed that there was 'such a good spirit when you think of all that people had to contend with' but the overwhelming impression is that of happiness and enjoyment. It was 'very intensive but very satisfying' and they all felt a 'great sense of privilege being there'.

CHAPTER ELEVEN

Eva's first five years at Howard came to an end. She had not had one day's illness during the whole time. Her appetite for life, boundless energy and numerous gifts and graces made her an all-round person. Even those who had never met her could tell from her letters and articles that she had something special; an eye for the kind of colourful details people would remember. Yet she was in no way stuffy or aloof.

'She was aware that God had given her much; physical strength and mental strength. This must all be used fully for the Lord. The word of Jesus had come to her as a great challenge. "To him who has been given much, much will also be required".'

Others were also well aware of her talents. In Africa she had enjoyed the company of men and many had come under her spell including government inspectors, colleagues from other teacher training establishments and senior staff working for one of the major publishing houses. If her dedication to the Salvation Army had faltered there would have been an abundance of other openings. Did marriage ever become one of those options? During her time in Rhodesia, Army magazines had been celebrating the centenary of Booth's own marriage and however dedicated his soldiers very few of the single women did not chafe against his restrictions when opportunity presented. How about Eva?

'There weren't really many single men around, and he'd have had to be a pretty outstanding young man to take her in hand.'

Back home in Australia it was a different story. Although it was her first furlough she was using it to study for her Master's Degree at Sidney University. Her striking good looks, keen intellect and attractive personality did not go unnoticed.

'I had to be careful lest I didn't say to myself "I've served God and done something for Him, now perhaps here is a relationship that will offer me happiness and marriage". I was so convinced of my calling so before it got that far I had to step back from the relationship.'

The fact that she was approaching thirty cannot have made the decision any easier. Neither can the marriage of her younger sister Margaret to Dr Bram Southwell, at which Eva was bridesmaid. Not that she begrudged her sister happiness, but it must have raised a few 'if only's ' in her own mind. Especially when the men still kept calling.

'I didn't realise how much I interested some men. I'm very much at ease with men. I like them. I never felt shy. Probably because I had brothers. But I would never have considered marrying someone I didn't admire greatly. Maybe a man older than myself. Someone I could look after. Who had achieved.'

Because of her loving nature Eva would have enjoyed having children and a family but feels it 'was one of the things God required me to give up'. During the last year before her furlough one hundred and seventeen new soldiers had been sworn in at the Howard corps. Teacher training was growing and expanding. She had been newly appointed Captain. There was too much at stake.

Once she was back in Rhodesia the issue faded in importance. If she mourned inwardly it did not show outwardly. She was not the dependent type and if she had to go it alone then so be it. There was nothing unusual or unacceptable about the single life. It was a vocation just as much as marriage and sometimes far less demanding. She could throw all her considerable energy into her work, which she had always found more than fulfilling.

'Some people go to work and they're longing for the job to be finished so they can have a good time. If work is enjoyable people seem to think there's something wrong with it – but if your work is also your joy you don't mind what time you spend on it. I really felt I'd given myself totally to African life.'

There was certainly little time to get bored. Garfield Todd, the prime minister of Southern Rhodesia, opened a new teacher training block at Howard in 1957, which increased the intake by 100%. Before that all the students had taken a course which qualified them to teach children for their first five years in school. Eva became the 'architect' of a new course – the Primary Teacher's Higher Course. This equipped the students to teach up to standard 6, an extra three years of schooling. The head of the college, Captain Lyndon Taylor, considered the pupils fortunate to have such a 'thorough and gifted teacher who made the most of her cheerful and vibrant personality'. In her spare time she managed to complete her Master of Education degree, writing a thesis on African education. Ingrid and other loyal friends spent long hours burning the midnight oil with her when it came to the final typing. It was worth it. Her expertise was gaining recognition. Longmans, the publishers, sought her advice when they were planning adaptations to African culture in a range of their texts. When Lyndon Taylor became Principal of the whole Institute in 1965 Eva was appointed to his old position. She was also invited to become a 'consultant to the government' on a special committee which was to begin discussions leading to a national council for teacher training. Her colleagues included a Roman Catholic principal of a teacher's college, an Anglican and a man who was starting a united mission teacher's college and had written several books on teacher training. It was considered a great honour not only for Eva, but Salvation Army work as a whole.

Sadly the beloved eldest brother, Beverley, who had poured cold water on the whole idea of Eva going to

Africa, was never to hear of her success. He died suddenly and unexpectedly of a coronary in 1962. He was only in his forties and had four children. Some years before he had resigned from the forces for their sakes and was personnel manager of an oil refinery in Perth. He was very much involved with charitable groups, attended the Salvation Army, and played in the band and the Perth orchestra. Eva's parents wrote her the news. It was a great blow to all the family.

1962 brought more shocks for Salvationists in Rhodesia. In September of that year 'many Army and church buildings were set on fire. In one area . . . four halls had their roofs burned off'. They were repaired or rebuilt within weeks, but local members often suffered verbal and physical abuse, not least for their involvement with the white people who were becoming increasingly resented. Many Africans now had an education. They wanted opportunities to participate in the decisions that were going to affect their country's future. The politicians made vague promises about independence. It was a long time coming. African writers began to question the motives of those who held the positions of power, including the various missionary organisations.

Looking back those who worked at Howard can see that the years from 1962 to 1969 were crucial ones. Some officers can now see that at the time they were 'typical colonialists' who failed to read the signs of the times or entrust positions of authority more readily to African leadership.'We thought there would always be a Governor General, and a European Prime Minister, that government would always be in the hands of Europeans and we would always be needed, and always be in charge. We knew very little of African political striving.'

As the secondary schools developed the discontent became more obvious. They became the spearhead of political disaffectation which was usually manifested in the form of strikes. Howard was not immune. If there was a grievance the students would refuse to eat their evening meal, and parade and make noises, or sit in a solid wall of silence. Debate became increasingly difficult, especially on the sensitive issues of race and politics. The overseas staff found the outpouring of resentment against the whites and the sense of disadvantage the Africans expressed hard to handle. Normally it didn't harm relationships in the long term but there were occasions when people could feel very hurt. 'We thought we were acceptable to the students. We'd given our lives for their advancement. It was something you had to accept, understand the reasons for and carry on regardless.'

Eva's feelings ran deeper. When she left Australia more than a decade before she had prayed that God would fill her heart with love for the people to whom she was to minister. God had answered that prayer, and taught her that the people had their own ministry to offer in return from the time she first set foot on African soil. Her conversations with the villagers as they shelled peanuts or sat around the fire, the interest she took in her pupils and their home backgrounds, her journeys out into the villages on teaching practice or corps activities had given her an appreciation of how the Africans thought and felt. She shared their hurt at the way they were sometimes treated, and was angered by the restrictions that were placed on them. Often for no logical reason.

'They could go to university and become nurses and teachers. But a boy could not become an apprentice to a bricklayer, or a tradesman. It used to hurt me that an African who was considered good enough to hand the cement to the man to lay the bricks couldn't get the opportunity to lay the bricks himself and become a qualified tradesman.'

When she went to South Africa on holiday she deliberately stood in the queue designated for 'blacks' at the Post Office counter, and left in disgust when she was told to queue in the area reserved for whites.

Rhodesia did not have an open policy of apartheid. They talked of 'separate development' or partnership.

But it was a horizontal partnership with the Africans invariably clinging precariously to the position of very junior partner. Even in the churches the Africans were often considered second class citizens and it was unusual to see an African in a white church. When Eva took some of her black students to play the tambourine at a big meeting in Salisbury it raised quite a few eyebrows and temperatures.

Eva would never have described herself as anti-white, but she was definitely pro-black. She had worked with Africans long enough to value their skills and ability and be totally incensed by studies purporting to prove that Africans were of lesser ability than Europeans. When Ian Smith made his Unilateral Declaration of Independence she was deeply troubled. She said:

'I felt at an earlier stage there were enough moderate Africans who could have taken their place alongside whites in government and there would have been much more evolution towards African leadership than the revolution that came about in the end. I'm against violence but I can see the logicality that people felt they had to fight to win their independence.'

Although not a political animal she saw the need to speak up for the Africans; articulate on their behalf when so often they were not given opportunity to speak for themselves. 'If I'd been in the political arena I'd have shouted. I have never changed my view that whatever colour or race we are there is this common humanity.'

While she was at Howard they did an experiment in teaching early mathematical concepts using simple material like seeds and shells. A professor came down from the university to investigate the project. A small black girl was weighing material on a balance. The university man put equal quantities in both pans.

'Which is heavier?' he asked the child.

She looked up at him, wide eyed at such ignorance.

'They are the same,' she replied. Wasn't it obvious for everyone to see?

CHAPTER TWELVE

Out on the compound, away from the news bulletins, those who lived and worked with the Africans often forgot that some were black and others white. On the whole they lived peaceably and had lots of fellowship together.

Eva never speaks of being afraid as the various political situations blew up even though at times it must have been rather like walking a tightrope after UDI. Because of the underlying sense of grievance numerous situations could have been interpreted as yet further evidence of white imperialism. Eva's 'terrific relationship' with the Africans carried her through. So many of them had been trained by her and trusted her friendship and judgements.

Her superiors were equally impressed. They had noted her attention to detail, especially business detail. In June 1965 she was appointed Vice Principal of Howard Institute, the first woman to hold the position. That same year the Salvation Army was celebrating a hundred years of witness in Rhodesia. Captain Eva Burrows took forty five corps cadets to the first corps cadets congress in that country. There were about two hundred and fifty cadets in residence and some of them had never seen cadets from another corps. Part of the programme included talks prepared by the cadets on the subject of the centenary. The Howard contestants gained first and second place, but what was 'especially gratifying was the note of pride in the Army running through them all'.

The following year Lyndon Taylor went home on leave. Eva had been working as his second for a number of years.

She was very able and 100% co-perative. In May she was asked to take over as acting principal for six months in his absence.

Administration was no problem. It might not be her number one priority but she had been organising people as long as she could remember. Organising your equals is a different matter. Internal promotions always pose problems and there were those who found her hard to take. Lyndon Taylor was a fairly relaxed leader. Eva would have had difficulty holding the reins, even for such a short time, without wanting to give them a short, sharp jerk occasionally.

In June she was promoted to Major. It was a lot to assimilate. There were all the different groups; nurses, teachers, agriculturalists, officers, students. Keeping a balance between the competing needs was a great test of leadership and she was still only in her mid thirties. However many feathers must have been ruffled in the process Eva survived and received a further vote of confidence in her leadership skills when she was appointed principal of Usher Institute, a girls' school with a growing reputation , south of Howard in Matabeleland.

Her new life at Usher started appropriately on January 1st. One day in the office, and she understood the situation better than some of the staff who had been there for years. It was her first opportunity to have unchallenged leadership. An idea she found exciting.

'I didn't have to take my ideas to somebody else and hear them say "Yes . . . but". I didn't blame other people for not being prepared to take the risk. But now I was in a position to have a go myself.'

She may have been more assertive for a while as she found her feet, but she is remembered mainly for the way she consulted staff and her obvious concern to do the best in every situation.

Her enthusiasm was infectious. The stones which marked the roads had to be painted regularly. There were no street lights, even though the development of the Kariba dam ensured a more reliable source of electricity in the buildings. One day Eva and another member of staff went into town on the weekly run leaving the maintenance man the job of painting the stones. On their return they discovered he had not only done as instructed but painted the trees which lined the drive as well.

Adjusting to her style of leadership must have been a learning process for not only the maintenance man. Getting used to an all-female environment must have been just as much a shock for Eva. She had always enjoyed men‘s company . Now she was surrounded by ‘girls, girls, girls – hundreds of them, working, playing, singing, laughing, crying, dancing , studying, lazing, praying.’ *(All the World,* pp66-67). Even the staff were women. Mrs Burrows wrote warning her daughter that ‘women are not always kind to each other’. Eva didn’t find it a problem once she had made the initial adjustment.

‘Women can give attention to detail and because we were not married we used to devote ourselves to the place. We used to have great times talking together. We’d set about improving the meals or the buildings. The girls’ uniforms were very smart – blue and white striped, so we painted the buildings to match; off-white with a blue trim and turqouise doors. A single woman gets her fulfilment in things like that – creating an environment as beautiful as possible – in which people can flourish. We tried to make it the best school, and it was an outstanding girls’ school.’

The main fly in the ointment was the maths results. When Eva arrived they were shocking. There was a general statement throughout Rhodesia that African girls could not do maths. Eva determined to prove it wrong. Besides her other duties she took over some of the maths teaching. One of the happiest moments in her life occurred when she was walking through the compound at Usher. One of the students called after her, ‘Major. Major’. There was a sense of urgency in her voice. Eva turned, expecting her to report some serious incident, like a bush fire.

'What is it?' she asked.

'I've just made up my own quadratic equation,' the girl panted triumphantly.

Eva had achieved another objective. Her aim had been to get the girls excited about mathematics, and to give them confidence in their own ability. She succeeded on both scores.

'They could do it as well as anybody else. No question at all. It was just that they'd been told they couldn't do it. I showed them that they could.'

Being in control of the finances of an organisation can pose a major headache for some people, especially if they are thrown in at the deep end with little or no training, which can happen in Salvation Army circles. Eva's knowledge of mathematics meant she could handle the budget at Usher with few problems – apart from the usual one of there never being enough money to do all that needed to be done. In a country where education had expanded so rapidly the gap between young and old had accelerated so teaching the adults to read and write was becoming urgent. Courses to train officers in these skills were planned at Howard and Usher. An article in *All the World* reported, 'There is no money for this but we are going ahead in faith.'

Buildings constantly needed to be expanded or replaced. Facilities had to be improved. In a land-locked country like Rhodesia with disease endemic in all streams and pools the opening of a swimming pool caused great excitement, even if all the money to cover the costs had not yet been raised. The inspector from the education department who could be such a trial came to the opening ceremony. He looked at the eager girls and the officers in their cream uniforms.

'I'll give £5 towards the funds if the Principal will jump in,' he challenged. Eva did not need to be asked twice. In she went, uniform or not, and swam right across. The girls gave a great cheer. They loved this exuberant officer who could laugh with them and join in their games, without losing any respect. They knew she cared. They also knew they had to behave. When a girl was caught stealing sugar from the kitchen she wept buckets at the telling off she received. Later she came back to thank the major for her punishment. If her father had been informed she would probably have been beaten. Another pupil was less direct. She claimed to have come from a different school but her story somehow didn't ring true. The officers felt they should ring the other school to check her story. The girl returned to her dormitory. A few minutes later a second girl ran into the office.

'She's swallowed a needle,' she sobbed. At first Eva and her assistant did not believe it, but the second girl was almost hysterical. They had no alternative but to take the cause of all the drama to hospital, forty miles away in Bulawayo. When X-rays were taken there sure enough was a needle. Instead of a place in school the girl had an operation.

Nobody expected the pupils to be paragons of perfection . The standards the principal expected of herself were a different matter entirely. While Eva was at Usher, General Coutts visited the country. There was a special event in Bulawayo, and Eva and a young Australian Salvationist had taught the girls a timbrel item to the accompaniment of a tape. They arrived for the performance only to find the tape recorder would not work. There were thousands of people waiting. What would they, and the General, think? Ingrid came to the rescue. Somehow she managed to improvise a tune on the piano, and the girls, with their natural sense of rhythm, adjusted to the new instrument without making the transition too obvious. Everyone breathed a huge sigh of relief.

Christmas came in the summer holidays and was celebrated with a simple feast and decorations of flowers or branches. Easter was the high spot of the Christian year. On Good Friday everyone would be very serious, and go about their business as quietly as possible. There would be an Easter play, though no one would want to play the part of Judas, that 'wicked person' who betrayed his Lord. Most of the action would be improvised with two or three scenes happening all at the same time as in a mediaeval play. One minute someone might be the donkey. In the next scene they could be the high priest. Easter Sunday morning the students would go round the bedrooms as early as 2am dressed in sheets, pretending to be angels, singing 'Christ the Lord is risen today'. When everyone was up and outside the school where it was hilly and rocky they would act out the resurrection scene, emphasising 'Christ is risen'. Then they would all dance and jump about, waving palm branches and getting wildly excited, till the air resounded with shouts of 'Hosanna, Hallelujah' and the equivalent in their own language. Breakfast was a special treat. The usual sazda would be replaced with bread and jam. On the compound they were never desperately short of the staple foods, though it was more difficult when sanctions were imposed during the Smith regime. Out in the villages conditions were much harsher. Usher was not far from the edge of the Kalahari desert and the local people often went hungry. With the help of Oxfam, a big outside kitchen was set up. The village children would come daily with their tins and dishes for a helping of sazda. Some of the secondary girls considered such goings on beneath their dignity but it wasn't long before they began to take an interest and help out in the 'Ox-farm'.

African rivers run underground for part of the year so the villagers would often have to dig in the sand until water seeped through. Usher relied on bore holes and tanks although even those proved inadequate one year when the school had to be closed for three months because of the shortage of water.

Bush fires were a further hazard. If anyone spotted a fire everything would come to an abrupt halt; lessons, services, meals. Then there would be a frantic rush to grab an armful of branches and beat out the flames. One evening they were out for a long, long time. They were all covered in ashes with thorns in their feet. The nurse from the clinic on the compound lined them all up to have their feet swabbed with disinfectant in case any of the thorns were poisonous, principal included.

While Eva was at Usher the political situation did not give them too much pause for thought. The girls were less politically conscious than the boys, although the staff would notice a more defensive attitude when the pupils came back from the townships after the holidays. At night though the girls could become more easily frightened and the regular checks on the dormitories increased in importance.

One day a member of staff found a man smoking in the girls' dining room. 'You're not allowed to smoke in here,' she said reprovingly. A few minutes later a police jeep screeched to a halt outside. Police and dogs tumbled from the vehicle. The man with the cigarette had been armed and wanted by the police.

Sadly the situation did deteriorate during the seven-year war and lots of schools closed as the troubles increased. By 1978 the overseas staff at Howard had shrunk to single figures. The staff at Usher were advised to leave the danger zone. Some declined the offer. In June of that year a group of armed men rounded up some of the teachers and started to take them down to the principal's house. On the way they were disturbed by a lorry. Panicked, they shot. Two young British teachers died. In an editorial some years later the Army magazine *Salvationist* reported, 'Diane Thompson and Sharon Swindells did not merely lose their lives . They gave them.' It was a tragedy, but in many ways also it typified the kind of commitment which has characterised Salvationists throughout Army history. Houses, land, family, self are of secondary importance. It is Jesus Christ and his service which is their goal and glory.

CHAPTER THIRTEEN

Ella Burrows was another example of dedicated service. She and Robert Burrows had served in twenty one appointments during their time as officers. They retired from active officership in 1957 but it is hard to imagine either of them not being still fully involved in whatever spheres of service were still open to them, including the all important regular letters to Eva.

Ten years after their retirement they were still writing. Eva had only been at Usher a couple of months and was preparing to go to the International College for Officers (ICO) in London on a refresher course after her long years overseas. She was just on the point of leaving for London when her brother phoned to say that their mother was dying. He was sending the money for her to fly home. Eva, who felt she owed all she was, and had achieved, to her mother did not take a great deal of convincing.

As soon as she arrived on Australian soil she went straight to the hospital. Mrs Burrows had been paralysed by a stroke. She could not move, speak or see. As Eva entered the room Joyce said, 'Darling, here's Evie'. Ella's eyes opened in recognition. After that all anyone could do was sit by the bed holding her hand. For the first time in many years all her surviving children were back in Australia. Before that Eva had been in Rhodesia, Margaret and her husband were doing medical missionary work in India, the boys had been in the Far East.

For two months the family watched and prayed. On July 8th, 1967, at the age of 76 Ella Burrows fought her last battle. Joyce, who had experienced more than her fair share of personal sorrow, described it as the saddest day of her life. She had been so close to her mother it was as though part of her self had died.

Once the initial surge of grief had passed the funeral was almost a celebration. Salvationists speak of death as 'promotion to glory' and Ella Burrows had a splendid farewell. She had been held in high esteem by numerous people who all wanted to pay their respect. At the graveyard there was a slight hold up in proceedings. The brothers had purchased a beautiful metal casket as a sign of their love for their mother. It was larger than usual and the grave had to be widened. Nothing daunted, the mourners moved over to one side and made the most of this grand reunion. It was a beautiful sunny Queensland day and there in the sunshine they rejoiced in the shared memories.

'Everybody said, "Well, there you are. She didn't want to die. She loved life. She didn't go down easily. And she was always bringing people together." There's this picture of life and vitality. Able to give and give to people without herself being drained. She was a great person.'

Because she was staying at home with her father Eva had the task of sorting out her mother's possessions and sharing them with the family. One thing stopped her in her tracks. Mrs Burrows had kept all the letters Eva had sent from Africa. There were no other papers. Just Eva's letters and a couple of clippings from the newspaper about her. Eva thought back over all the times her mother had encouraged her. The sacrifices she had made to ensure her education. The continuing support through her training and years in Rhodesia. The pride she had shown when Eva had been asked to speak at meetings when she was home on leave. If Eva had any regrets it was that her mother had never been able to put in words just how much she obviously meant to her, and that there had not been more time to spend with her parents over the years.

Furloughs went by so quickly. There was always so

much to do. Even now the weeks were passing. She was long overdue at the ICO. She was torn between staying with her father and going to the remainder of the course. Her father insisted she should go.

It was a healing experience. One of the special provisions God seems to keep tucked up his sleeves for times of particular need. The ICO was housed at the Cedars in Sydenham, south London. There were fine old trees, sloping lawns and a view over the hills of Kent. The wooden panelling and stained glass windows created a genteel air from a bygone era. If the lady of the house had swished down the stairs in a crinoline en route to her waiting carriage it would not have seemed out of place.

The principal, Commissioner Gattrell, was a woman of great spiritual sensitivity and gentleness. She was a fine preacher, not in a declamatory style, but 'the kind who would shine at retreats, and extremely well read'. Eva began to realise her own spiritual diet had been very meagre in comparison. Every morning there would be a prayer time which was introduced with quotations from the great Christian classics; Mother Julian of Norwich, de Caussade, St Theresa of Avila. Eva the activist was learning to 'Be still and know' the God who speaks not only through action but in silence and meditation. It left her with a great admiration for the contemplatives, even if God still has to forcibly take her by the scruff of the neck and put her in a position where she has no option but to be still on occasion.

The few brief weeks at the ICO opened her mind to an appreciation of meditation literature. It also reopened her awareness of a world beyond Rhodesia. She loved Africa and the African people. Now new horizons were being presented. People were commenting about her gifts and abilities. She was asked, 'Why don't you come and teach in London?' She found the mixture of nationalities at the ICO stimulating. For the first time she began to wonder if she was to be given leadership beyond the context of Africa.

It was a preparation for what was to come. Up till then Africa had been her life. She was happy there. It had not occurred to her to seek for anything else. Now the seeds had been sown. She was not one for planning or manoeuvring but confidential reports are kept on Salvation Army officers throughout their careers. They are not tremendously significant unless a person's name comes up for a more senior position. Eva had already been promoted to major before the usual time. Senior officers were obviously watching her progress with extreme interest. Notes would have been made and observations passed. She had undoubted ability.

She also had enough at Usher to occupy her mind without fretting about future possibilities. Her philosophy has always been to give her best to the job in hand: 'If that is well done everyone will want you on their team.'

Unknown to her, requests were already being made for a transfer. A few days before her fortieth birthday she received her farewell orders. Her time in Africa was coming to an end. When the day for her departure arrived nobody could be heard for the weeping and wailing of the girls. 'It was very traumatic. I was like their mother. I was a strong disciplinarian. If a girl had exceeded the way she should behave I would send for her parents.'

Parental authority was strict. Eva had no hesitation in continuing the tradition. The girls knew exactly where they stood.

'Ah, but mufundis you are a real father to these girls,' declared one elderly parent whose daughter had stepped out of line. Major Burrows had dealt with the matter so effectively the father did not need to administer any further punishment.

Mother? Father? However they viewed her the girls knew that her love was genuine, and the discipline was a necessary part of the love. They would miss her greatly. The feeling was mutual. Leaving Africa was an immense wrench. As a child the continuous moves had taught Eva to leave behind the place they had been and give herself to the new. This time round it was not so easy. She accepted the fact that she was probably ready for further responsibility but at that stage she had no idea what the responsibilities would be. She was simply sailing back to Australia surrounded by the accumulated baggage of the last seventeen years. Africa had been a significant part of her life. Now she was leaving for good. It was like a bereavment. More were to come. She knew her father was ill, but didn't appreciate how seriously until she arrived in Perth. A sister in law met the boat.

'You'll have to get off the boat and fly,' she said. 'Dad is really ill. We don't expect him to live.'

Eva was used to acting under authority. She did as instructed, going straight from the airport to the hospital. Major Robert Burrows had cancer, but Eva's arrival seemed to give him a new lease of life. The doctor was so pleased with his progress he said the patient could go home if Eva was going to be there to look after him. She was able to care for him for two months in the small cottage which had been her parent's retirement home.

'I felt very privileged to do that. All those years I had been away. Those last two months were a great joy to me.' Of course there were bad days. It is not easy watching someone you love die, and Robert Burrows went through a phase of doubt and anxiety which is part of the process of letting go but can be particularly hard for Christians to accept. Eva's strong faith and reassurance in words and song took them both through, despite the double blow of the death of her eldest sister Dorothy only a month before her father died.

'We loved Dorothy. She was so generous. Even when she'd married and left home. She lived in the country with her husband and she was a great cook. Everybody knew when they went to her place they would always find tons to eat. She'd give away her last penny. She was almost profligate in her generosity.'

There had been three deaths in the family in as many

years. Eva spoke or sang at all three funerals. In between clearing up her parent's affairs she was doing deputation work, visiting various places to speak about the work in Africa. It must have been like rubbing salt in an open wound. Her own future was still uncertain. The ties with the past difficult enough to sever already. Eventually she had word she was to 'proceed to London'. She still had some of her holiday left so she decided to go via America and visit some of her former colleagues en route. The day she left Australia she was informed her new appointment was as vice-Principal at the ICO. The uncertainty was over. The full sense of loss had yet to sink in.

CHAPTER FOURTEEN

'The first six months at the ICO were definitely a period of strange readjustment.' In a sense Eva had suffered a triple bereavement; the death of two members of her family in close proximity, and the loss of her beloved Africa with all its warmth and colour. The grey streets of London and a Western society on which the permissive 1960s had made its mark were small compensation. The grasping acquisitiveness of an affluent society were a further shock.

'I'd identified so much with the Africans. I thought, will I be able to communicate with these people? Cultural differences are very great,' said Eva.

In *The school of charity,* Evelyn Underhill draws a parallel between the changes that take place when the Holy Spirit is working in us and the effect of yeast on dough. The texture changes and the loaf of bread is completely different to the original lump of dough. If the dough could feel the yeast working it 'would be very painful'. Eva Burrows was undergoing a similar transformation though people talking to her probably understood very little of what was going on inside. 'It was uncomfortable. It was a changing time in my life.' Anyone who has had to work through the shock of bereavement will identify with the emotional upheaval involved.

The change in status could have done little to help. At Usher she had been top dog. Now she was back to being second in command. Commissioner Gattrell was no longer in charge. Neither was Eva Burrows. It must have been something of a shock to her system. Then there were questions about her style. Some of her mannerisms and charismatic approach to leadership were not always appreciated by the conservative British. She had been used to teaching in a country where English was the second language. If people were not to assume she was talking down to them she had to speed up her presentation and tone down her air of authority.

'I think they thought I didn't observe all the rules of protocol – but I didn't know them. . . They were patient with me. A bit of a brash Australian,' she said.

All these were minor details. It was customary for the group at the ICO to visit local corps a couple of times during their visit to Britain. Twenty years on people still remember those visits. All Eva wanted to do was communicate the gospel and make the meetings 'interesting and bright'. She did that, and more. Contemporaries describe her as 'outstanding', 'stunning', 'she really hit the London scene.'

The dark hair was now highlighted with silver. Naturally. Not out of a bottle as some undoubtedly imagined. Like her mother, Eva was to be grey by her mid-forties. It only served to make her look more distinguished. She has never used a great deal of make-up. She doesn't need it. Her features are pronounced enough already, and much of her attractiveness lies in her sense of style and good grooming.

'I always think that Christians shouldn't look dowdy or fuddy duddy. I used to laugh when you read books about missionaries with bobby sox and funny old clothes. No decent shape. I've always tried to dispel that idea.' She succeeded. When she first arrived at the ICO the reaction was identical to that on her arrival in Africa: 'Wow. What have we here?'

Eva was less concerned with the impression she was making than getting to grips with the new job. She was not dealing with novices. To qualify for a course at the ICO officers must have done a minimum of ten years' service. There would be approximately twenty four in each group from eighteen to twenty different countries. A list of delegates for July 1973 includes officers from Belgium, Brazil, Canada, India, Korea, South Africa, Switzerland, Zambia and the four zones of the USA. There were no exams or diplomas. They were there to learn about the world, the church, the Army, themselves. The aim was that they might go back to their home territories 'further equipped in mind and spirit for the tasks to which they are appointed'. As assistant principal Eva was responsible for a great deal of the curriculum. After her experience in Africa she could almost do that standing on her head. Prayers required more sensitivity. Commissioner Gattrell had set a high standard. She had retired in 1970 and married General Coutts, a 'scholar and man of wonderful insight and perception' at the age of sixty five. Eva used much of her material supplementing it as time went by with quotations she had discovered in the local library and the library at the ICO.

Her most valuable contribution lay in the relationships she built up with delegates from all round the world. During her stay at the ICO nearly five hundred officers came under her influence. Eva took those from the developing nations particularly under her wing. She was able to appreciate the problems they might be having dealing with English spoken in a variety of accents and dialects after learning it in a purely academic setting. After the lectures and discussions she would spend extra time ensuring anyone with language difficulties had grasped the important points.

During free time she would make sure everyone had sufficient to do. She would take groups to concerts, or to other churches so that they could listen to preachers of different denominations and widen their experience. Her time was at the delegates' disposal. She had left Africa behind. Now she was gaining a whole new world view. She was learning as much as she was teaching. The two principals she served under were men coming to the end of their service after long experience as leaders. She regarded them as 'mentors' who taught her a great deal about management, and international leadership. The students were all leaders in their own right. She had to find a balance between the role of leader, inspirer, companion, friend. Group dynamics were a great eye opener. It was fascinating to watch how people of different temperaments and races worked together or to observe the way key personalities tended to colour the group. One group might be labelled exuberant, the next 'the quiet ones'. Always the strong personalities had great power of influence.

Eva continued to make her own personal mark. Like most organisations the Salvation Army receive a number of tickets to the Royal Garden Party each year. When Eva's name was suggested for one of the invitations she was thrilled. Her various leadership positions had already given her opportunity to meet people of power and influence, but she was not so blasé that she wasn't delighted to be going to Buckingham Palace. Once there she spoke to several people including the Archbishop of Canterbury. 'If I'm going somewhere I don't just stand. I had some interesting conversations.'

A sudden movement of the crowd was more disconcerting. Bewildered, she asked what was happening. Someone explained that the royal family were coming. She must stand in line to leave an aisle for them. Eva found herself about four rows back, wondering what was to happen next and chiding herself for not thinking to check beforehand. A gentleman in waiting was walking down the aisle. Behind him came the queen. He appeared to be inviting various people forward for an introduction. He caught Eva's eye and beckoned. Somewhat overwhelmed Eva straightened her uniform and moved forward.

'What do you do?' enquired the usher. Eva told him.

'That's very interesting,' he replied. 'I'll introduce you to her majesty.' Eva gathered her wits together. She must concentrate hard so she could report in full detail when she got back to her eager students. The queen nearly destroyed her efforts. She looked so beautiful in a dusky pink outfit.

The usher explained that Eva had been working in Africa and was now principal of an international college. The queen asked how the groups got on coming from so many different backgrounds and cultures, and if they were making any new recruits.

'I was quite amazed at her being able to use the terminology that suited the Salvation Army. When I went back to the college everybody was thrilled that I'd had a chance to meet the queen.'

Eva claims it was her uniform that got her noticed. It is certainly known as a symbol of 'availability' in many nations. It wasn't the only common factor to emerge during the various forums at the ICO. Whatever the cultural background one characteristic went right across the board: the desire to evangelise. Eva had seen it in Africa, grown up with it in Australia, was learning about it in Asia. Japan was a complete surprise.

'I saw Japanese Salvation Army officers who were really enthusiastic evangelists. I'd expected them to be quiet and reserved in their style as they are seemingly in their culture. The psychologist Jung speaks about racial unconscious and I suppose in every race there is this something that we call racial characteristics, but on top of that there are other influences you take on board. We often speak in Africa about the conflict of cultures but there can also be a merging of cultures. In a sense the Salvation Army is a subculture. We get built into the fabric of national being.'

A Kenyan widow, Mrs Captain Asiema, illustrates her point. At the end of her eight-week course at the ICO she declared that the experience had been like a very deep well with pure water. She felt God had given her 'a long rope to draw up the water to nourish her soul'. When people queried whether Eva's alert mind would get bored repeating the same course every couple of months she had a ready answer. How could she get bored when people and their circumstances were so fascinating?

'She was marvellous in that position. She was excellent at getting to know people, especially in one to one relationships. Many leaders haven't got that genuine interest.'

She also had a considerable advantage. A memory that can slot a name to a face or situation almost instantaneously. What about closer, personal relationships? There was chance to renew acquaintances with families she had known in Africa. Was that closest of relationships still to be denied? Eva talks rather of finding fulfilment elsewhere. A great deal of her life was 'given to the delegates'. There was little free time to get to know people in Britain in any depth. Other possibilities were opening before her. The move from Africa to London was a significant landmark. She was getting a good response from her students. Her potential for future leadership was becoming increasingly acknowledged: 'That was a rich satisfaction to me. If you're not going to marry you must feel that there's opportunity to use the gifts and abilities you have.'

During a fun evening at the end of one of the courses the students indulged in a little teasing of the staff. They presented the principal with a big badge marked 'Order of the Founder', one of the honours for distinguished service in Salvation Army circles. Eva they decked out in the gold trimmings for a General, set on a pink velvet collar with a lace edge. Never one to stand on her dignity, 'General Eva' joined in the frolics holding the Army flag draped across her body like the first General Eva while the cameras flashed.

To her it was all good fun. Others took such things more seriously. Her family had never doubted she was heading for the top job. Before Major and Mrs Burrows died various Army leaders had told them 'You know that one day Eva will be General?' In 1972, the year another brother, Walter, died after many years illness, Joyce came to London to spend six months with Eva. Wherever she went it was the same story. Many, even a retired General, all forecast the same event. Joyce thought back to the prophecy of 'Fighting Mac' forty years before: 'One day we will have another Evangeline in this little girl.' It looked as though his words could be coming true.

CHAPTER FIFTEEN

Eva had been at the International College for Officers for five years. She was now principal and 'fully involved' in devising new ideas for an administrative course for potential Third World leaders. When she was called into the General's office in the rebuilt International Headquarters in Queen Victoria Street only a couple of hundred yards from St Paul's Cathedral she had no premonition that further moves were afoot. The General was seated at his desk. The chief of staff (his second in command) was by the window overlooking the river Thames. Obviously something important was about to be announced. Before Eva had time to do a mental check list of any way that she or the students at the ICO might have offended, General Wiseman informed her that he felt she was the right person to take over leadership of the women's social services. Not many things manage to shock Eva Burrows. That certainly did. She wondered if he was saying it with a question in his voice, testing her response. It went against the grain but she must query the wisdom of such a suggestion.

'Never in my life have I questioned an appointment,' she said, weighing every word. 'And if you are giving me that appointment I will go. But I've never had any experience in this field. I've been in education. I wonder if I'm really the best person for the task.' The General assured her they had thought long on the matter, and had decided not only that it would be a suitable appointment for her, but that she had much to contribute to social services.

Eva left the room in a state of shock, saddened by the prospect of leaving the ICO just as the new initiatives were getting off the ground. A six-week furlough in Australia did little to lessen her unease. She had taken the opportunity to read so much about the social work of the Army she felt she knew the history, background, areas of special need inside out – in theory. How she would handle the top job when so many others had years of working experience in the service was a different matter.

The staff at social services had similar reservations. Who was this Eva Burrows who was being appointed over their heads? Most of them had seen her at meetings or heard of her in connection with the ICO. She obviously had something about her, but her sphere was education. In Britain social services run independently of main line activities. Social service leaders worked their way up through the system. The current one had served in hostels, children's homes, approved schools and as district officer for many years. Why appoint an outsider? reasoned her officers. What did the staff at headquarters think the rest of them were doing? Standing on their heads? It felt like a vote of no confidence in them. They might as well give up on the spot.

The six weeks in Australia were a good move. By the time Eva took up her new appointment the ruffled feathers were somewhat smoothed. Far from finding hostility she felt people were very receptive, and her second in command was so competent Eva continued to puzzle over her own sideways move. It must have been a delicate situation. Here was someone in the top position virtually starting from scratch as far as the day-to-day running of the various institutions were concerned. When she tried to lay down the law experienced officers found it hard to stomach. Nevertheless they swallowed their wounded pride and did all they could to help if she asked for advice. 'She just went out of her way to get to know what was going on.'

The staff were amazed at how quickly she grasped the various issues and was able to slot them into the incredible filing system of her memory. That, and the sheer magnetism of her personality, won the day. She had only been in office a fortnight when she gave a lecture on social services at the ICO. An officer who had worked on the social side for twenty years summed it up as 'the most brilliant lecture on our social services I'd ever heard in my life'.

Mistakes there must have been. Eva admits she 'may have been a bit impetuous in those early days', but she was always willing to learn, and apologise when she realised she had overstepped the mark. Far from not knowing what she was doing her staff discovered it was all they could do to keep up with her. She had a 'tremendous capacity for absorbing work', often expecting others to achieve the 'impossible yesterday'. Those closest to her were never aware of her not working. Even when she was travelling she would be checking she had all the facts at her finger tips for her next assignment. On one occasion she planned to fly up to Scotland for a meeting about the children's work. She was talking over the details with one of the leaders in Scotland by phone beforehand.

'But that wouldn't apply up here,' said the Scottish officer, Beth Groves.

'Why not?' queried Eva.

'Because the Children's Act in Scotland is just that bit different to England.'

'Why hasn't someone told me this before? I'll ring you back.'

She did, to say she was no longer travelling by air the next morning. She was going on the overnight train so that she could read the Children's Act of Scotland en route.

She did her homework thoroughly, reading profusely. Government reports, social legislation, anything she could lay her hands on that would better acquaint her with her work. It was just as well. Army social work had nearly as long a history as the Army itself, dating back over ninety years. Booth's command to Bramwell 'Go and do something' was still the dynamic. Ten years before the turn of the century Booth had written a controversial best seller,

In Darkest England and the Way Out. He claimed that if the state neglected the poor the public had a Christian duty to fill the gap. His vision included slum brigades, lodging houses, eating houses, legal aid and the first labour exchange. It was seen as a 'literal attempt to apply the Christian ethic to industrial civilisation'. (*The General Next to God*, Collins) Many of his far-reaching proposals only came to fruition during the social reforms after the Second World War.

Despite the many improvements in state provision Eva found her time at social services a great eye opener. As she talked to key people and travelled round Britain on her preliminary fact-finding tour she discovered she had a big area of ignorance. She had been aware of poverty in the Third World. Now she was finding the affluent West had its own poor and destitute: 'There are so many sad and lost people – psychiatric, emotional, problems of insecurity and alienation.'

At the time women's social services had over seventy centres including hostels for the homeless and mentally ill, mother and baby homes, provision for the elderly, children's homes and community homes for difficult teenagers. The budget ran into millions and staffing was always a nightmare. Catherine Bramwell Booth, the eldest granddaughter of the Founder, had discovered when she was head of women's social services fifty years before that the leader needed a thorough knowledge of Salvation Army policy and practice and a keen grasp of government legislation. Things hadn't changed much. A large part of Eva's day would be taken up with letters, phone calls, management meetings, finance boards, councils, and committees. Weekends would be spent 'Specialing'; taking services in various corps and talking about the work. She had to be able to liaise with the local authorities, professionals in the social services, and people with specialist knowledge who worked on the Advisory Boards. A sound financial department and her strong sense of accountability enabled her to understand and monitor the financial side. The public areas were no problem. 'She is a public person. She enjoys that side of things. With her personality she shouldn't be behind the scenes.'

If she was standing in a doorway people couldn't but be aware of her presence. The effect was even more dramatic when she swept into a meeting. People would hardly be seated when she would start to run through the various points, hands waving in explanation, face live with enthusiasm. She had a tremendous gift for making people see their own potential and do things they never dreamed possible. One timid secretary with very little self confidence was instructed 'Go out and get yourself a driving licence. You're no good to me if you can't drive a car.' The secretary did as instructed and passed the test first time. She drove Eva to one of the community homes where she was due to address a group of girls. One of them slouched in her seat making a great show of what she thought of the event. 'I don't know what your name is,' rapped Colonel Burrows. 'But I'm not talking to the top of your head. Sit up.'

The whole row sat bolt upright. Eva was definitely an autocrat. People didn't argue unless they had good cause, and a fair amount of courage. When Colonel Burrows was around there was no mistaking who was in charge. People followed her leadership. Newcomer or not. It stood her in good stead when it came to the areas of change which are always necessary in an organisation approaching its centenary. For a start many of the buildings were nearly as old as the organisation. They had a Dickensian air with enormous dormitories and little privacy. They needed to be upgraded or adapted to current needs. There was too much living in the past. Not enough awareness of the modern era. Eva did her best to 'spark everybody up' and probably trod on a few more toes in the process. It may have been painful but she got things moving. 'She was a tremendous pusher. If she knew a thing ought to be done she would really push hard.'

Sheltered housing in Scotland, upgrading of hostels, adapting premises, such as mother and baby homes where there was less need, to shelters for the victims of violent homes – which was a growing problem – all received pushes in the right direction under Eva's capable guidance. Much of it was paper work, assessing a need and arguing its cause. Would that remove her from the ordinary people? Far from it. When she visited the hostels and goodwill centres or was out on the soup run distributing food and blankets to the homeless on the streets of London, the caring side of her nature came fully into play: 'I think something of my mother came back into me.'

Just as Ella had cared for the poor and the prostitute whom no one had wanted to know so Eva began to appreciate feelings she had only known before in her work in Africa. A century before William Booth had seen the need of the 'submerged tenth ' of Britain whom nobody else seemed to care about and declared 'These people are our people.' Eva was in total agreement:

'I admired so much our officers who lived all the time with the women in the hostels. Who would bath them when they came in filthy. The soup, soap and salvation of an earlier era. So many things were required of them, especially among the women who were alcoholics. A lot of their love would be rebuffed or thrown back in their faces. Yet these lonely, unhappy people needed to know there was somebody who loved them.'

Eva often tells the story of a woman in one of the big hostels in Scotland that she was visiting just before Christmas one year. The officers had been telling her about this particular woman who was very lonely. No one appeared to take any interest in her. By the side of her bed there was a locker with one Christmas card. 'She's got a friend somewhere,' Eva remarked, pointing to the card. 'No,' came the reply. 'She sent that to herself.'

As Eva went into the hostels she realised the Salvation Army was not there to turn people into converts, but that their work must be an extension of Christ's love: 'Jesus

Christ didn't say to the man who was filled with many devils – the schizophrenic – "If you follow me I'll cure you". He just met the need. We are in social work to meet people's needs.'

To Eva, like generations of Salvationists before her, those needs included the spiritual and the social. There was no dichotomy. They could have modern hostels, improved facilities. There would still be those who would find their consolation in the bottom of a bottle or continue a restless search for the love they had never known. 'You change the location,' says Eva. 'You don't change the person. You improve the facilities. You don't change the problem.'

All you could do was show warmth and love and affection, and continue to 'be there' to pick up the bits. There would always be critics who would see it all as a carrot to attract the donkey. Maybe with some justification at times. A woman living 'under the Army's care in London' thought differently. In a paraphrase of the twenty third psalm she wrote,

The Lord is my Warden; I shall have a roof over my head.
Tonight I shall lie down in clean sheets and blankets.
And, if I am lucky, have a good night's sleep.

A local authority supported her verdict. When one of the women's social service homes was under threat of closure they suggested, 'Don't close yours. We will close one of ours . . . You give social service with a plus.'

Inevitably there were stresses. Anyone who works close to the darker side of human nature cannot help taking on board some of the pain. Social services HQ was based in Mare Street, in a rundown area of East London. A far cry from the leafy suburbs of Sydenham. Time out was essential. Epping Forest, a vast tract of woodland made available to the people of London by Queen Victoria, provided a much needed source of refreshment. Eva could go walking there the weekends she was free, capturing the beauty of the beeches or a snow scene in detailed photographs, a hobby she had first taken up in Africa. The sight of a twig she had picked bursting into bud in a vase was enough to send her in raptures.

She had a similar effect on people. At an officers council two of the lads got up to sing a duet at a free and easy sing-song after the intensity of the day. Before they started they unbuttoned their tunics. Across their T-shirts was printed, 'I love Eva'. Eva joined in the hilarity as much as anyone. She has the rare gift of being able to take a joke against herself, and her command of words and easy rapport enable her to come up with a quick response to most situations. When a colleague threatened 'I could write a book about you. I've seen you with your hair up and your hair down,' Eva had an instant answer: 'You be careful, my girl. I've seen you with your rollers in.'

CHAPTER SIXTEEN

The fifteen months Eva spent at social services were all too short. When orders came to a new appointment there were regrets all round. She was sorry to leave. The staff who had greeted her arrival with such scepticism were sad to see her go. She had achieved much, and given them all an injection of hope with her sparkling personality, keen interest in their concerns and positive reactions to even the most difficult situation. One of her last acts was to present a dossier recommending that the men and women's social work should merge. It was obvious to her from the beginning that there was too much overlap. By stating her views on the way out she could not be accused of empire building on her own behalf.

Not that she had need to. She had enough on her plate. The new appointment was Territorial Commander for Sri Lanka, a pear-shaped island to the east of India. Its lushness and tropical variety made it a place of great beauty with winding roads and hair-pin bends giving spectacular views over the jungle. Legend held that once a year an angel came to dance on the highest peak.

Homestead gardens produced spices, vegetables, coconut, kapok, breadfruit, mangoes, cashew nuts, pawpaw, plantain and pineapples. From the sixteenth century a series of colonists had realised the economic potential of the area and established plantations growing cash crops such as tea, coffee, cocoa, rubber and pepper. It was a land of contrasts; sunshine and torrential rain, poverty and riches, ruins of ancient civilisations and all the problems of unemployment and inadequate health care associated with a newly independent nation where population outstripped production on a regular basis.

The complicated cultural, religious and political make up created a further cause of tension. The prejudices had built up over centuries but had become more accentuated since independence in 1948. There were two main cultural groups: the Sinhalese and the Tamils, and four main religions. In a population of approximately fourteen million, ten million were Buddhist, two million Hindus (mainly Tamils), one million Muslims and one million Christians. It was one of the toughest commands, and Eva's first experience as a Territorial leader. 'I thought – oh gosh – a whole new situation, an entirely new culture, new languages.'

Did she despair? On the contrary. She took herself off to the library, read all she could, and ordered a set of language tapes. Army work had begun in the island in 1883. Early Salvationists had waded through snake-infested swamps, stripped to the waist, and established huts thatched with palm fronds. Almost a century later there were five thousand Salvationists in sixty five centres, still battling against the poverty and disease which had so concerned the first arrivals.

Although a comparatively small group, the Salvation Army or Galavima Hamudava in Sinhalese and Ratchaniya Senai in Tamil, had an influence far beyond their numbers because of their social work. It included beggars' homes, hostels for children and working girls and care for the elderly. With her experience in social service in Britain fresh in her mind the new Territorial Commander took a particular interest in that sphere and was soon rallying support from the far corners of the earth. There were plans to re-develop headquarters. Phase one would mean moving senior citizens to another part and developing a worship centre, hostel for business women and community centre with day care for children, and a feeding programme for the poor. Phase two would concentrate on headquarters and the development of the building for commercial purposes. What did General Brown in London think of the plans? The Salvation Army in Canada was celebrating its centenary around the same time as Sri Lanka. Could they be persuaded to help? And Sweden?

The Salvation Army in Sri Lanka had a reputation for making a rupee stretch further than anyone else. Eva Burrows was in her element continuing the tradition. 'I built a new home for senior elderly ladies. I enjoyed that. It was my first experience of being totally responsible for trying to get funds, selling people the idea and overseeing the building.'

Like her mother, she had a good combination of practical shrewdness and strong faith. When money was required she would calculate resources, inform people of the need, then go ahead trusting that God would move people to respond. She no longer needed to jump in the swimming pool to raise £5, though if it had been necessary she would probably have done it:

'You believe in God but you also use every means possible to raise funds. There are a lot of inter-relationships of fiscal principles with Christian principles. I used to receive money from people I never even knew. Quite often I would open my post and there would be a gift from someone in Australia or Canada or America.'

They needed chairs in one of the village corps worship centres. A man in Canada wrote to say he had heard of the problem and was going to send a hundred dollars every month. Eva was over the moon. A hundred dollars would fill the church with chairs. She wrote to thank him. Some months later he wrote again. He had been to the mercy seat and wanted to be a soldier, but there was a problem. He smoked. Would they pray for him? If he could give up smoking the Army in Sri Lanka would benefit by another one hundred and thirty dollars a month. Colonel Burrows rallied her troops; the people in the property council, the villagers who could now sit in comfort. Their main concern was not that they should receive the extra money but that the man's desire to give up smoking would be met. Several months later out came the two hundred and thirty dollars and a message: 'Your prayers have been answered. And so have mine. I've given up smoking and I'm getting enrolled as a soldier.'

It all took time but often it was the personal touches that reached people's hearts. The letters, postcards, the silver tray in the shape of the island Eva sent to her personal secretary back at social services in London. She has always considered people to be of prime importance no matter how elevated her position.

In May, 1977, it moved another step higher. General Wiseman was retiring and a High Council had been called to elect the next General. As Territorial Commander Eva qualified to attend. She was forty seven and the youngest member since Commissioner Catherine Bramwell Booth had made her reluctant appearance at the first High Council. It was back to the books to find out what to expect. General Orsborn had written that at a first High Council newcomers should keep quiet and listen to what people say. It might not come naturally but Eva determined to follow his advice. Her plans were overthrown the first day when the president requested that she should be chaplain. Eva pointed to her age and inexperience. The president was not to be deterred.

'I was up nearly all night because I had to lead the first devotions at the High Council, with all those experienced and senior leaders of the Army world.'

True to form, her talk was practical and to the point. She shared the perplexity she had felt as a young officer when she first discovered that a certain number of votes were required to elect a General. In her innocence she had assumed that when all those wise and holy leaders came together the Holy Spirit would put one name into all their minds. Colonel Rive, Principal of Howard, had set her mind at rest, by showing her a verse in Proverbs: 'Men cast lots to learn God's will, but God himself determines the answer.' (Proverbs, 16, verse 33, Good News Bible)

They were at the High Council under the guidance of God. He would make His will known, however diverse the instruments and seemingly haphazard the events which prepared the way. As illustration she referred to an incident in Sri Lanka. Some work in the inner city was being oversighted by a widow with several children. Eva could see great potential for future development but feared that the added responsibility would be too much for the widow on top of the double load she already carried. The chief secretary warned of the trouble it could cause if Eva moved the family. She prayed. No other solution seemed possible. She decided a straightforward chat over a cup of tea was the next move.

'How are you getting on?' she asked the widow in some trepidation when they met. 'Well,' came the hesitant answer, 'I'm finding it very difficult here. I know you will be disappointed but I really would like you to give me a change.'

God had worked out a way which showed the futility of human manoeuvring. Eva needed the knowledge of that power beyond her own to cling on to over the next few months.

In June, 1978, two girl Salvationists were killed at Usher during the unrest Eva had foreseen if the Africans were not given leadership. Soon after Sri Lanka experienced another series of riots and communal disturbances which left thousands of refugees in temporary homes. A Hindu family lived in the house next to Eva. Every morning she could hear them singing their mantras with the children. When rioting broke out Eva was concerned for their safety knowing that all the other neighbours were Sinhalese. She went to see if she could be of any use. Offer the loan of her car? But the family's goods were already loaded. They were eager to be on their way. Their car had hardly turned the corner when the mob arrived and smashed the house to pieces.

January, 1979, brought a different kind of disaster. A cyclone came across India, over the north of the island and down the eastern side, causing complete devastation. In that area many people relied on the coconut plantations for their livelihood. 'I shall never forget it. The coconut tree is so beautiful. It's got graceful fronds. It was as if an angry giant had come along and just clipped off the trees,' said Eva.

Eva and her emergency team were amongst the first on the scene taking in food and clothing, and assessing the need for financial aid to help rebuild the shattered homes and schools. One particular incident is indelibly printed in her memory. As they drove past a massive fallen jak tree a man and his two sons were digging out the trunk. They were fishing people and were obviously hard at work fashioning a new canoe. Eva observed:

'No matter how devastated people can be there's a tremendous resilience in the human being that allows him to get up and start again. I never felt we were just handing out things. These people were already showing that they were trying to make the best and rebuild their lives.'

A week later she had news that an elderly Salvationist in the central area had died. He had expended himself so much for the people Eva made the long journey to his funeral as a mark of respect. It was one of the saddest she had ever attended. The rain had not stopped for days on end. The houses were in shambles. The grave water-logged. Yet there was no weeping and wailing as is the usual Sinhalese custom. Just a quiet acceptance and payment of tribute. 'I had a great sense of the worth of a simple person's life and service to God.'

If it gave Eva pause for thought it certainly didn't show in any relaxation of the pace she set herself. Many had found to their cost that Sri Lanka could be very demanding physically. The intense tropical heat was debilitating and Eva wasn't as wise as she should have been about her health. At Howard she had hardly known a day's illness. Why should Sri Lanka be any different? Less robust persons might need a siesta. Not Eva Burrows. Besides, how could she pause to rest in the middle of the day? There was too much to do. The evangelical work was particularly challenging. No one could convert to Christianity in Sri Lanka without a complete break from their family and culture. The usual aggressive tactics of the Army had to be somewhat modified. 'I learnt a new tolerance to other faiths. I could never come to the situation where I would say we're all equal. I cannot do that because of my belief in the pre-eminence and uniqueness of Christ. But I learnt to respect other religions.'

Not that it stopped her talking about the Jesus who was the centre of her life. Whether it was to her own Buddhist cook, or when she was invited to do a series of 'Thoughts for the Day' on the radio. As she listened to other speakers, Hindu, Buddhist, Muslim, she realised there was great similarity. They all spoke about conduct, morality, ethics. She was going to speak about a person, who not only walked this earth two thousand years ago, but walked beside his followers in the twentieth century. And carried them a fair portion of the journey: 'The thing we have that is different from every other faith is that Christ is a living Saviour. The Buddhist says "You walk in the noble path." Christ says "I am the path. I'm with you".'

She also took her own soldiery a step further. They were often in danger of forgetting that the good news they heard each Sunday had to be applied to everyday life if it was to have any validity. The preparations for the centenary were too good an opportunity to miss. Maybe they could be used to build up the spiritual life. Plans were set in action for the upgrading of publishing and education programmes and rejuvenation of the soldiery as well as the more obvious building and social programmes. The first soldiers' Congress within memory took place while Eva was in Sri Lanka. The two fast-paced days were full of concentrated teaching on spiritual revival, uniform wearing, goal setting and stewardship.

As a cadet Eva had taken Colossians 1 verse 18 as her special verse: 'That in all things Christ might have the pre-eminence.' When she was appointed Commissioner, second in rank to the General, in July, 1979, someone left a gardenia, her favourite flower, on her seat at the thanksgiving service. Alongside it was a card with a handwritten reminder of the verse.

She appreciated the nudge to her memory. It is all too easy for someone in a position of influence to think they are there simply by virtue of their own ability. In Salvationist circles there may always be a reminder to 'Give God the glory'. But Eva was making her mark in much wider spheres. She was active in the Sri Lankan Christian Council. The president was a great Anglican bishop, bishop Lakshman Wickramasingha, a highly educated man with great Christian faith and a strong sense of social justice. Before long he recognised Eva's ability and invited her to be vice president. She protested. She was a foreigner and already had more than enough to do inside her own organisation. He assured her the job would not be too demanding. It was a purely nominal position. He already had one vice president. Eventually Eva agreed. Within months both president and the other vice president were off on study tours. Eva was left to handle the chairmanship. To make matters worse a crisis in the Council came to a head. Eva drew a deep breath, arrowed a quick prayer, and went to see all the people involved. She was able to act as a reconciling agent in a way no one could ever have foreseen. She was neither Sinhalese or Tamil and she was known not to take sides.

The ordinary people loved her. She identified with them, spoke up for them, tackled situations others had avoided. Her talks were so simple even little children could listen and understand. Many of her ideas were innovative but she could convince those in authority of their value, and carry them through. When she knew the plans were afoot to move her on her concern was for her second in command, a Sinhalese whom she considered worthy of being leader. With so many major projects in hand she wanted to make sure that everything was in a fit state. There was the rebuilding programme at HQ, the centenary celebrations, plans for a regional college for officers from India, Pakistan and Sri Lanka, modelled on the ICO. It had been her first real taste of top leadership. All the loose ends must be tied up.

'I was glad to have a second chance to be leader to correct some of the insensitivities that I may have had, because of my own personal drive, wanting to get things done. And done well. To a high standard. I may have been too authoritarian. . . I think if I'd been in a Western country I would have had a lot more comeback . . . To balance that out they knew that I loved them.'

Indeed they did. When she left Sri Lanka in September, 1979, the comment column in the *Ceylon Observer* paid her a great tribute. 'Eva Burrows is a foreigner. She is a Christian which by silly standards should cut her off from the people in our predominantly Buddhist country . . . We ought not to think her departure worthy of editorial attention. Who really cares about the Salvation Army? Who really cares about her work in Sri Lanka? Who cares whether Eva Burrows stays or goes?

'We say without fear of contradiction that people like Eva Burrows grace any country they serve in. They do not proceed to ask what is your religion before they serve. They only ask in common humanity what they can do, and proceed to do it . . . Sri Lanka will miss this woman, Eva Burrows,'

CHAPTER SEVENTEEN

From Sri Lanka Eva went to Canada for a world conference of Salvation Army leaders. Then it was back home to Australia for a bit of 'spoiling' from the brothers and sisters. They had always done their best to help Eva switch off during her breaks – taking her to the Great Barrier Reef, Tropical Tablelands, coast, islands – wherever they could manage. This time they evidently thought she needed a bit of fattening up. The brothers, who now had good jobs, took her for meals where she could eat her fill of exotic sea foods and rich desserts. Eva, who has always enjoyed her food, made the most of it.

Sri Lanka had been a tough assignment. Next on the list was Scotland. She arrived to the 'whirl of pipes and sound of drums' in November, 1979. The Salvation Army had celebrated its centenary in Scotland that year. The arrival of their first woman leader was extra cause for excitement, especially one with family connections. Robert Burrows had been born in Dundee. Eva was halfway home in their hearts.

Despite the divisions between Catholic and Protestant in cities such as Glasgow the Salvation Army have always been held in affection in Scotland. Their long track record of social concern spoke for itself. In his centenary greetings to the Army, the Secretary of State for Scotland paid tribute to their 'massive contribution in the field of social welfare'. Eva was coming in at a high spot of the Army's history. They were receiving a fair amount of media attention. She had hardly been in the country a month when she had the privilege of speaking on TV during a midnight service from George Square, Glasgow, on Christmas Eve. It was a bitterly cold evening but the warmth of the greetings she received on the streets over the next few days made up for it.

'You're the new Salvation Army lady.'

'Hope you're going to enjoy it here.'

'Welcome to Scotland.'

Eva's charm was having its effect on even the supposedly dour Scots. Lord Wallace of Campsie, chairman of the Glasgow Advisory Board, had viewed the appointment of an Australian woman with some trepidation. His foreboding quickly turned to enthusiastic support when he saw her in action.

As Territorial Commander Eva was responsible for all that happened in Salvation Army circles. She appointed officers, kept a watch over financial affairs, and made sure the work was progressing smoothly. At weekends there were preaching engagements and visits to the various corps. She was the one who was expected to liaise with civic authorities and heads of other churches. In theory it was mainly a public relations job. In practice it involved an enormous amount of administration also.

Her second in command, Lieutenant Colonel John Hounsell, was a walking encyclopaedia of Army rules and regulations. Eva was exceedingly grateful for his expertise. It was the New Year, always a busy time in Scotland. Lots of places to go. People to see. They had a bad day in the office. A number of unexpected things happened and in the middle of it all they had to make a decision about purchasing a property. By the time evening came Eva was asking 'Is it like this every day?'

A former colleague from Usher saw her and thought she looked very thin. Sri Lanka had obviously taken its toll. It was a good job Eva had such a strong physique. There was no cause for alarm. She was never ill.

Eventually the day came to an end. Eva went off home to finish unpacking her suitcases. Her new secretary was arriving and was going to share her flat for a while. Everything must be spick and span.

At 4am the secretary's sleep was shattered. Eva was in agony with tremendous pains across her chest and shoulders. 'I think I'm having a heart attack,' she explained with an effort. Two of her brothers had died with coronaries. She knew the symptoms. She had not even been in the country long enough to register with a doctor. What should they do? Speed was essential. Neighbours told them to ring the hospital. Within minutes an ambulance was on its way.

All Eva remembers is lying on the sofa wondering if she was going to die, and saying, 'Well, Lord, if this is the end of my life I'll just have to say how thankful I am, and what a wonderful privilege its been, but if it's your will for me to live then I just give myself to you all the more. To the best of my strength.'

The next she knew she was lying in a room with one of the students from Usher standing by her bed. 'It's allright, major,' the girl assured her as Eva struggled to make sense of her surroundings. 'I'm going to look after you. You've done so much for us.'

Eva was in hospital, in the intensive care ward. The girl who spoke to her was doing a postgraduate course in nursing. Eva took it as a sign that she was going to get better. Others were less certain. Her mind was alert enough. Even in her semi-conscious state she had been able to give them the phone number of her sister Margaret in Australia. But her body had taken a battering. For several days she was allowed to do little more than lie and listen to the radio, almost disappearing under an avalanche of flowers and messages from all round the world. There were postcards of an African village, breakers crashing on an Australian beach, a frond of orchids from Sri Lanka. One envelope included the heading 'Ward 12B, International Centre of Prayer'. It was very appropriate. Eva felt the prayers were already proving powerful.

Eventually she was moved onto the General ward. The

gifts kept rolling in. A giant basket of fruit drew everyone's attention. 'Who sent that?'

Eva read the card. 'Lord Wallace of Campsie.' There was a stunned silence. Two pots of cineraria caused further incredulity. They were from the Lord Provost of Glasgow. Eva hastened to explain that she did not normally move in such exalted circles. These were simply two of the many influential people who supported the work of the Salvation Army.

Sunday brought more diversions. One of the Army bands came to play in the ward and an orderly rushed in, waving a newspaper. 'Oh, Miss Burrows, your picture's in the paper. Real nice too.' Eva was somewhat surprised to find herself considered a celebrity on account of a Sunday paper. All she had wanted to do was make sure her followers knew she was back on the road to recovery and fit enough to joke 'the Scottish people have so amazingly walked into my heart the impact has been far more powerful than I could have imagined'.

They continued to do so. Her diary details her fellow patients on the ward and people who continued to hold her interest even when she was far from well. Such as Agnes and Flora, two 'unknowns' who sent her a postcard because they had seen her on 'telly' and were sorry to hear she was poorly; eighty-year-old Phoebe who kept them awake one night when she was in a distressed state; the flower lover who treated the ward as a potting shed taking clippings from the various plants; the 'blether' of women she was invited to join round one of the beds when she was fit enough to take a short walk. Eva's understanding of Glaswegian was expanding rapidly. She had no choice. Even the consultant greeted her with 'And how's the high heid yin of the Salvation Army today?'

The treatment was only what any patient recovering from a heart attack would receive but the quiet authority of the bushy-browed doctor commanded the respect of staff and patients alike. Eva, who was more used to giving than receiving orders, determined she would do as he said. She knew she had misused her body in Sri Lanka, pushing it to its limits in the tropical heat with inadequate time for rest. With hindsight she could see it had been unwise, especially in view of the family history of heart disease. Margaret's husband was a doctor. He sent her all kinds of literature about heart attacks and their prevention. The message was sinking in. The consultant emphasised if she followed his instructions implicitly there was no reason she should not return to full health.

It was all that Eva with her positive personality was waiting to hear. She took gentle walks each day. She rested. She pruned her diet drastically, cutting down dairy produce and other foods high in cholesterol. She had never been a tense or anxious person. One of the doctors reckoned that the fact that she had not fought against the attack but handed the outcome over to God could well have saved her life. The sticking point was work. She maintains the 'only' thing she did on business while in hospital was answer letters, which, given the number she received, must have kept her occupied for a fair portion of the day. The remainder was taken up with minor details. Like keeping a diary. A regular pastoral round. Studying the names of Jesus in the New Testament. And managing to sniff out of her second in command a crisis back at the office, even though he tried to steer the conversation well away from work.

It was impossible. That agile mind was not going to sit back and take things easy even if her body had no option but to obey the doctor's orders. She is first to admit she would be an extremely difficult patient if she could not read or think.

Did she ever ask 'Why? What next?' Berate the Lord for giving her so much only to frustrate any future hopes? 'When I was recuperating I naturally questioned. The Lord seemed to say to me "You're pushing too hard yourself. Let go. Let me".' It did not come naturally. Those who took a 'negative line', warning 'You mustn't do this. You shouldn't do that,' got short shrift. Eva was convinced she would get well if she was sensible but she had no intention of spending the rest of her life wrapped in cotton wool.

If she lived – well and good. If she died – so be it. She would rather go out with a bang than a whimper. She had spent her life in service. She was not going to spend the remainder watching others do the work.

'Isn't that a bit selfish?' chided a colleague whose opinion she respected, and who stood more chance than most of applying the brakes. Eva's eyebrows arched questioningly.

He took a deep breath. 'Well, if you go on like you're doing now you may live only a few more weeks or months. If you steady yourself a little you could be giving the Army and the Lord a good many years. And you may one day be the future leader.'

There was a deathly silence. Had he overstepped the limit?

'Oh,' said Eva. 'I've never seen it that way before.'

Not that it seemed to make a lot of difference. Eva determined she would 'live every day as a gift from God'. She still managed to pack more into them than many fit and healthy people.

Her sister Margaret flew over. Those who were closest to her were going to make sure she did not take that gift for granted. Coming from Australia to the 'frozen north', Margaret had only one question as she stepped from the aircraft. 'Will I see snow?'

There were several precious weeks together, walking, talking, enjoying the quiet beauty of the Scottish countryside near the convalescent home on the Clyde estuary. Margaret's gentle presence was a healing in itself. A Sri Lankan girl, Prema, came to help in the house for a while. Beth Groves who had worked with Eva in social services did not take too much persuading to come out of retirement into the post of housekeeper. She knew Eva's worth, and her own brand of quiet determination was the perfect foil to Eva's 'get up and go' philosophy. She would make sure she did not go too far, or too soon.

Within three months Eva was champing at the bit. The doctor had said she could go back to work. They would need breakfast at 7am.

'As early as that?' queried Mrs Groves.

'Yes. I'm going into the office tomorrow.'

'But not before 8 o'clock surely?'

'I always go early.'

'But not after being off sick.'

'Why not?'

'Well... what about the other folk? They won't be in that early. It could be very embarrassing for them to arrive and find you already there.'

Beth Groves won that round.

'That's her,' she laughs. 'I'm starting work. Wham. Straightaway. Right on the jot.'

By Easter Eva was presiding over the annual weekend houseparty of the nurses' fellowship. That autumn she opened three new centres on three consecutive days. Eva Burrows was back in harness and delighted to be there. The social work was familiar territory. During her time at social services she had overseen much of the work, and had been involved in some of the preliminary work setting up housing associations to help provide much needed accommodation for the elderly. She had already met some of the inhabitants in the hostels for homeless people in Glasgow and Edinburgh. One group still fell through the net. There was little or no provision for the 'gutter' women; the heavy drinkers who slept rough. During the worst of the winter weather one was discovered dead at the bottom of a rubbish chute in a high rise building. Eva assessed the situation. 'Then I really got cracking and said "We've got to do something".' They provided plastic sheets and blankets in the local citadel and the women had a temporary shelter.

Many were drunk when they arrived. Jeannie Kennedy could outdo them all. Most days she 'drank herself into stupidity'. Like most of the women she had a man friend.

They form a partnership. Help each other. Jeannie's friend was dying. He had some money saved and wanted the Army captain to look after it for Jeannie. The captain agreed. After the man's death he told Jeannie of his gift, and said he would give her a little at a time so she didn't drink the lot in one enormous spree. A couple of days later Jeannie went to the captain. She wanted her money. In full. The captain remonstrated, but eventually he had no option but to give it to her. Before long she was back again. Could she borrow £25? The captain pointed out she had just spent all her friend had left her. What was she going to do with this money?

'I wanted to give him a nice gravestone,' she said. 'But the man needs another £25.'

The story was confirmation of all that Eva had learnt from her parents.

'People seeing Jeannie would say that's a woman who's sunk to the lowest depths, the dregs of humanity. But no matter how low a person sinks somewhere there's a spark of goodness that love can light up. We believe there's still hope in everybody. Even people with big alcohol problems.'

Social work was not her main sphere in Scotland however. Much of her time was spent travelling, getting to know people in the various centres, encouraging the evangelical work of the local corps. Sometimes she 'shocked the saints'. At a thanksgiving service her second in command was waiting at the top of the steps for one of the leaders to arrive. His car drew up outside. So did Eva's. Eva was out and up the steps before the other leader, greeting her deputy with an affectionate hug and kiss, much to the surprise of the man who was still climbing the steps.

Other times people got distinctly hot under the collar. Eva was never afraid to speak her mind, and she had an uncanny knack of putting her finger right on a problem, much to some people's discomfiture. One officer was convinced his superior had spelt out the situation in his corps in detail, so accurate was her diagnosis when she preached.

Wherever she went she was held in high esteem. Her charismatic personality and drive were 'putting the Army back on the map'. The provost of Glasgow gave her a nickname. Effervescent Eva. She could certainly bubble over on occasions but it was never a one-woman show. Whether she was talking to a pauper or a peer of the realm her interest in the other person was genuine. She made them feel they mattered more than anything else that was going on around. If she was addressing young people she made it her business to acquaint herself with their interests. Even to the extent of watching 'Top of the Pops'.

Lords and ladies came equally under her spell. Lord Thurso was the lord lieutenant who receives the Queen Mother at the Castle of May when she visits. Every harvest festival his father had taken him to the Salvation Army hall in Thurso and was generous in his support when the Salvationists needed to rebuild their hall. The present lord carried on the tradition, helping to raise money for the work with a big concert at which the Queen Mother was a special guest. When Eva first visited the corps as Territorial Commander Lord and Lady Thurso were there to receive her. Uncharacteristically, Eva got to the platform only to find that her spectacles were not in her handbag. She had left them in Glasgow. Lady Thurso looked in her own bag. She had a spare pair, which saved not only Eva's eyesight on that occasion but throughout the remainder of her tour up to Shetland. Later that same year Lord Thurso found himself in a similar predicament in Kelvin Hall, Glasgow. This time Eva offered the loan of her spectacles. When it was Lord Thurso's time to speak he was able to joke 'Your Territorial Commander and I see eye to eye.'

Although she was following in the footsteps of some very good leaders Lord Thurso felt she 'never languished in the shade of her predecessors, but brought her own style of freshness and enthusiasm, backed by a deep and secure christian faith'.

She was also one of the few Salvationists to see the need and value of the media. Most were reluctant, defensive, or simply hesitant to blow their own trumpet. Eva was more used to making her presence felt. While she was in Scotland she went on Late Call a good number of times, and took part in a series entitled 'Come wind, come weather,' in which various people were interviewed about crises in their life. In May, 1981, Eva celebrated thirty years as a Salvation Army officer. The *Sunday Mail* voted her 'Woman of the Week'. Only a few days before an ITV programme had been far from complimentary about some of the Salvation Army hostels. The natural instinct was to scuttle for shelter. Eva met the storm head on. The morning after the programme the whole centre spread of the *Record*, the Scottish equivalent of the *Daily Mirror*, carried factual details and photos of the Scottish hostels, supplied by Eva's staff. 'As far as Scotland was concerned that was the end of any backwash from that particular programme. She got off the ground so quickly with her public relations it was squashed almost before it came to life.'

When Pope John Paul II visited Scotland, Eva was among church leaders formally presented and was photographed greeting his Holiness with the Salvation Army salute. A finger pointing skywards. Unaware of the Army custom, the caption in the *Daily Telegraph* stated that Colonel Eva Burrows was making a 'feminine point'. Correction followed a day or so later when *Telegraph* readers were told that the upturned finger had been employed in early-day meetings when congregations sang:

The way to Heaven is straight and plain;
Will you go?
Repent, believe, be born again;
Will you go?

Eva was delighted to see this message in the daily press though she was less than enthusiastic about a Bill going through Parliament to ban street marches after disturbances with the National Front and the Orange marches. The Army had fought enough battles about their right to be on the streets at the end of the last century when Salvationists had been imprisoned, ridiculed, despised and attacked by hooligans. They would happily ask for permission if they intended to organise a big march through a major city. They had no intention of applying for a weekly permit to play on the street corner in every town throughout Scotland. Eva marshalled MPs, various lords and ladies, any of her friends in high places who sympathised with the cause, to lobby in their defence. The Bill was amended.

The Army's right to go on the streets is only one of the issues on which Eva Burrows has strong opinions. If people take an opposing line she will listen, is willing to learn, but there is rarely any doubt who makes the eventual decision. In Scotland she was known for her 'push', her ability to spark off ideas in those with a similar mental agility, her determination to get things done. Even after her heart attack she would work till midnight and beyond. Getting her out of the office was a constant headache. At meetings she was nearly always the last to leave. As long as there were people to greet, families to enquire about, matters to discuss she was happy. If she couldn't be found after a meeting people were always instructed 'Try the doors'.

She had to be doing something, either work or study. Relaxation meant filling in a crossword, or occupying her mind with a game of Scrabble. Car journeys weren't just occasions for surveying the scenery. They meant chance to catch up on work, or a book. Difficult journeys were a challenge, not a problem.

Not long after her arrival in Scotland she had to attend a New Year meeting in Aberdeen, far to the north over mountainous country. The previous year her chief secretary had travelled home on black ice and thick snow. He did not relish a repeat performance, and made arrangements to stay overnight. Eva took a different line. She wanted to go straight back. Eventually they reached a compromise. If the roads were clear when they came out of the meeting they would travel back that night. The meeting finished. The weather was damp, but there was no sign of snow. Eva was jubilant, thinking, see how you limited yourself when you did not think positively. Less than twenty miles out of Aberdeen they ran into a blizzard. The snow was so thick you couldn't even see the signposts. Her second in command who was driving was none too happy.

'What's so difficult about driving in snow?' enquired the intrepid Australian.'Let me have a go.'

It was perhaps as well John Hounsell had been given some forewarning. When Eva was appointed to Scotland one of the top leaders informed him 'You'll be teaching a future General of the Salvation Army how to run a British Territory.' What he did not say was that the 'future General' might have quite distinct ideas of her own on the subject.

Soon after Eva's heart attack the General of the day, Arnold Brown, who was a warm friend of hers, was talking to a group of officers about his work. With the word of the General absolute and discipline high on the list of Army priorities he inevitably came to the subject before long. 'Most people take notice of me, ' he said, 'but,' looking pointedly in the direction of Eva, newly returned to work. 'some people don't.'

If she had thought for one moment he was serious she would have been deeply shocked. In her mind she was acting under the highest orders – to give and serve and take up her cross daily. Her sense of discipleship went right to the root of her being. And it showed.

Writing in the Commons Diary in the *Arbroath Herald* in January, 1982, the MP Peter Fraser commented about a meeting with Eva Burrows. 'Every now and again you meet someone you immediately know is out of the ordinary. I doubt if I shall meet anyone else in 1982 who will so powerfully impress me as she did.'

CHAPTER EIGHTEEN

A few months later Eva was acting under a new set of orders. She was appointed Territorial Commander of Southern Australia. In comparison, Scotland and Sri Lanka had been like cutting her first teeth. The Southern Territory covered the whole of Australia, except New South Wales and Queensland, stretching from the Huon valley in Tasmania to Darwin in the far north. In area it was one of the biggest commands and had never been led by a woman. How would the 'macho' Aussie male cope with a sheep shearer's granddaughter heading up one of the most popular of the charitable organisations? Would Eva still be able to relate to an Australia three decades away from that of her own frugal childhood? The 'Australian dream' centred so much on material things; a good home, two cars out front, and a barbecue and pool out the back. Did anyone still listen to a message that put material things far from the top on its list of values?

In Salvationist circles the Australian soldiers were known for being smart, inventive, go-ahead. They were riding high on the morale boost their centenary celebrations had given them two years before. But even Jesus had found that 'A prophet is respected everywhere except in his own home town.' (Mark 6,verse 4 Good News Bible) Could the new commander expect a similar fate? Eva took comfort in a verse from Romans. The passage described Abraham's continuing faith as the years rolled on and the longed-for son had still not arrived. The neighbours might mock, Sarah get more and more sceptical. Abraham clung on to God, 'being fully convinced that God was able to do what he had promised' (Romans 4, verse 21, RSV)

On her first morning at Territorial Headquarters in Australia Eva was greeted by the staff. As part of the welcome the chief secretary read from the *Soldier's Guide*, a book of daily Bible readings written in the 1890s. The reading contained the very same verse Eva had claimed as her own.

'It was as if God was saying "It's OK. I'm going to be with you".'

Within a fortnight she felt as though she had never been away. Her speech, her mannerisms, the sense of belonging were more and more reversions to all that had been familiar in childhood. It was good to realise that she still had a home after all the years in other countries.

The same could not be said for some of the men she met when she visited a men's hostel in Melbourne. Many of them had never got back into the full stream of life since the Second World War. They were lost, lonely people with serious drink and drug problems. Eva spoke at a Sunday morning service. It was not compulsory but attendances were high. The men enjoyed singing old familiar tunes like 'Tipperary' and 'Irish eyes are smiling' even if the words Salvationists put to the tunes were 'religious'.

Afterwards one of the men came up to Eva.

'You know, Commissioner you spoke real ocker.' he said.

Eva took it as a great compliment.

'That's real Australian, fair dinkum Aussie. Most people probably wouldn't like to be told they speak ocker. It's a bit slangy. The common speech of the man in the street.'

William Booth had instructed his officers 'Use words that Mary Ann will understand and you will be sure to make yourself plain to her mistress.' (*The General Next to God,* Collins) Martin Luther had 'looked in the mouth of the man in the street' when he was translating the Bible. Eva Burrows was in good company . She had no reason to be ashamed of her origins. They could be put to good use.

'Though my speech is not broad Australian I'm recognised as Australian and I like that.'

An 'ex-pom' on her staff described Australians as kind, loving, hospitable though they were unlikely to be impressed with 'stuffed shirts'. He felt Eva's temperament contained all the best qualities; the openness, friendliness, energy, enthusiasm. With one important extra. She got things moving.

Each year in Melbourne there would be a conference of the heads of departments. The exchange of ideas was useful but nothing much ever came of them. The first year Commissioner Burrows put in an appearance they were discussing the training of officers. 'Right,' said Eva at the end of the session. 'I think we've talked about it long enough. Let's do it.'

It was quite a time before some recovered their sense of equilibrium after such a shock. They were in for more. Eva was 'an impatient sort of person. Impatient with anything that is mere talk, not action, and impatient with anything that is less than the best.'

When her brothers and sisters heard her in action they were stopped in their tracks. She was so like their mother. But Ella had only the local corps and nine children on which to expend her considerable ability. Eva's had been honed and refined by years of international experience: 'She really set about that territory.'

The centenary paled in significance. Eva brought things alive for the first time in twenty years. She had spark and colour. Her energy was boundless. It was difficult to believe she had ever had a health problem. She moved at such a whirlwind pace.

One of her first tasks was to get the Territorial Headquarters into shape. People had hesitated to do anything for years. The necessary building and refurbishment would run into millions of dollars. Eva saw the need, took account of the cost and chivvied folk into action.

Her financial advisers held their breath at times. Eva was no spendthrift but she believed in making money work. It should not sit idly in the bank when there was so much else it could be doing. In many ways the Army's vision has always outstripped its resources. There is a delicate balance between faith and foolhardiness. As a young woman Eva had been impressed by the way William and Bramwell Booth had often pressed ahead with projects and found the necessary funds arriving in the next post. If the need was urgent enough Eva was prepared to take similar risks. It had worked in Sri Lanka. Why not Australia?

A hostel for the wives and children from violent homes was an obvious cause in need of urgent attention. It gave families a roof over their heads but precious little else. The officers in charge had even had to prop up part of one wall so it would not collapse. They appealed to the government for funds but nothing was forthcoming. Eva decided they must go ahead. The financial secretary was less enthusiastic. As usual Eva stuck to her guns. A week or two later fresh funds came to light which could be used for such a purpose. Eva's faith was vindicated: 'I have a healthy respect for money, but I'm not over awed by it.'

She also has a strong sense of accountability. In Australia the public have always been very generous to the Salvation Army. People trusted them. Eva insisted there must be no gimmicks in their publicity. Nothing to destroy their credibility. She had no qualms about asking the public for help so long as Salvationists were doing what they said they would do. Their overheads were minimal. They took salaries and allowances far below others in social services and administration. They lived in a communication-conscious world. They needed to be 'in there', shouting about their work.

There was plenty to shout about. Australian Salvationists were among the first to be involved in welfare provision. When John Gore launched the movement in Australia from the tailboard of a greengrocer's cart the religious part of the meeting was followed by the invitation 'If there's any man here who hasn't had a meal today let him come home with me'. Australia might have been the 'lucky country' for some. For the old, the sick, the widowed, and unemployed it was far from the case. The Army's first social work was started in Melbourne and the Victorian government was the first in the world to give the movement a grant. Since then they have never looked back. There may have been criticism of the big institutions, dissent within and without about the best way of dealing with social problems. On the whole the Army is regarded with affection. Their work with alcoholics and drug addicts through the Bridge Programme has led to them becoming the recognised authority on alcoholism. Old style institutions are giving way to community care. New projects for the elderly include three-stage care, with a retirement village, sheltered accommodation and a nursing home on the same site. Individual corps are doing their bit to combat the loneliness and isolation which is so often the lot of many immigrant and single parent families in the downtown areas of the big cities. The Salvation Army is perhaps best known as the organisation which is 'always on the spot' in times of emergency. People have long memories. They do not easily forget the Robert Burrows of this world who gave them comfort and counsel during the war, or in the floods and fires which are a fairly regular occurrence .

Eva had been in office only a few months when bush fires in Australia hit the international headlines. On Ash Wednesday, 1983, the premier of Victoria, faced with many dead and thousands homeless, set disaster plans into operation. Salvation Army halls were piled high with gifts of food and clothing, and switchboards became jammed with offers of help. Commissioner Burrows suddenly found herself responsible for three million dollars people had sent to the Army because they believed 'You are the people who'll use it correctly'. In the area where the fires were raging even the police hitched lifts with Salvation Army relief teams. They were often the only ones allowed through the barriers.

Unemployment created an area of need which did not hit the headlines with such spectacular impact but could be equally devastating. Government provision might fend off the worst blows. It did not shorten the queues applying for food parcels and vouchers. Research and practical experience showed time and time again that the root of the problem was not scrounging but subsistence. Benefits were simply not high enough to keep a family adequately fed and clothed. The Salvation Army would carry on handing out food parcels because they could not bear to think of children going to bed hungry. They would also continue to put pressure on the government on behalf of the 'new poor'. Armed with the facts and figures provided by the research department and her own special concern for the disadvantaged, Eva Burrows launched into the attack. Traditionally the Army has fought shy of political issues. Eva took a line she considered apolitical. 'It didn't matter which political party was in power she would speak out on behalf of people who were getting a rough deal.'

The Salvation Army saw too much of the social consequences to be easily convinced by purely economic arguments. Far from alienating the government, Eva was asked to put forward her views at a tax summit in Canberra in 1985.

'Poverty is not just having a low weekly income or a social security benefit,' Eva pointed out to the assembled gathering.' It means having a lack of cash left after paying the rent, a lack of capital for satisfactory housing, adequate diet and sound health, a lack of good credit standing. Then when a family crisis arises or there's a sudden health problem the poor have no resistance, no escape from the vicious circle that imprisons them.

'It is the responsiblity of the government of a country to see what revenue is needed, and what priorities need to be addressed, then to structure a tax system which will obtain that revenue and not exploit the poor whom it was designed to aid.'

William Booth had championed the cause of the forgotten class, the 'submerged tenth' of British society at the end of the nineteenth century. Eva Burrows was doing her bit on their behalf as the twentieth century drew to a close.

She has never lacked the courage of her convictions. With a research team keeping her supplied with information on all kinds of moral and social issues she did not hesitate to stick her neck out on such subjects as *in vitro* fertilisation, gambling and prostitution. If other churches combined efforts on a certain issue so much the better. If they didn't she could always use the pages of *War Cry* to present a case, or badger public persons with letters, reports, questions and well-documented information.

Having spent so many years of her life with young people Eva was particularly distressed to see the effect unemployment and the break up of family life were having on the youth of Australia. Living close to her own family once again, especially her sister Margaret and her children who had always had a special place in her affections, was a great pleasure and delight. In 1985 she officiated at the marriage of her niece Jane; another Eva according to those who know her. Despite the years apart the family ties have always meant a great deal to the Burrows clan. Eva knew she owed so much to her own secure upbringing. She identified enormously with the families in the low income bracket. She could not stand by and watch a generation of youngsters sink into lethargy and despair.

A factory-based programme called Employment 2000 was set up to teach job skills, increase self esteem, and provide a continuing interest in the youngsters when their thirteen week course finished. Eva did all she could to support and encourage it, and to rally her fellow Salvationists' enthusiasm for the cause.

On one of her first visits to the corps at Fitzroy in Melbourne she discovered another project worthy of attention. The officer was responsible for a homeless youth centre attached to the corps. Eva was impressed by the warmth and friendliness, and the good sense of home, but shocked by the condition of the building. 'If it's the last thing I do I'm going to see a proper house built for this work,' she declared.

It was not easy. Government restrictions, Army traditions, and local opposition were formidable hurdles. Eva persevered. She was prepared to put her muscle – which was considerable to effect if it would move a few mountains.

CHAPTER NINETEEN

A Prime Minister of Canada, Arthur Meighan, described the Army as 'a vital spiritual force with an acute social conscience'. In Australia, as in many other areas of the world, the public were often aware of the Army's social work, but did not appreciate they also had a spiritual ministry to offer. Young people especially tended to see the Army's music and traditions as firmly embedded in the nineteenth century with little relevance to the new objects of worship – the sun, self and success. Numbers were declining.

Commissioner Burrows summed up the situation in a press interview in her first week in office. Australia had become materialistic and secular. People were forgetting the spiritual dimension to life. She would like to see revival in the church. She set about getting it. The church growth movement had been successful in the States. Would it transplant to Australia? Or the Salvation Army? Was church growth inspired by God as Eva believed the origins of the Salvation Army to be, or was it just another gimmick? She sent two officers on a study tour to Canada where church growth was already quite prominent in Salvation Army circles. She read books on the subject till it 'was coming out of her ears'. The more she read the more excited she became. The language might be different but the principles and aims were almost identical to Salvationism in its hey-day at the end of the last century. The use of the laity, the place of the pastor as an organiser, personal witness, small groups, identification of spiritual gifts, the re-emphasis on the place of the Holy Spirit; evangelism was the key word. Not the massed rally format but personal, individual, local. An 'each one bring one' philosophy. Apparently 85% of newcomers into church had come as the result of personal invitation. If statistics like that didn't fire Salvationists nothing would. The officers who had visited Canada shared Eva's enthusiasm. Seminars were set up. Church growth officers appointed. People began to wake up to the possibilities. A divisional commander introduced a 'friends and neighbours' day in his area. Local corps were encouraged to put on a service which was geared to people who would not normally come to church. Everything had to be interesting, fast moving, short. It was publicised on television. Salvationists were warned: 'Don't come unless you bring a friend or neighbour.'

It was so simple it was ridiculous. And it worked. Many Salvationists were forcibly reminded that evangelism was not just the prerogative of the officer. It was a requirement for each of them. People began to question how they could apply church growth principles in their own locality. Did they need to alter times of services and open airs? Put more emphasis on Bible study and less on the band? Meet in less formal house groups? Think about teaching materials and follow up? The Salvation Army had always been quite good at encouraging decisions. Unfortunately those who made them didn't always take them any further: 'We were saying not only decisions, but disciples.'

The young people began to sit up and take notice. Here at last was something they could do. And see the reason why. This Commissioner Burrows actually took note of them and their culture,and would ask, 'why haven't you got a rhythm group?' rather than 'what's that terrible din?' You could talk to her at meetings. She wanted to know what plans the youth secretary had for the future; the new initiatives young people had for evangelism. If someone suggested a 'religious night club' she listened intently. She didn't throw up her hands in horror.

Die-hards took a bit more convincing. The very concept of a woman in a position of authority had been hard enough for some. The staff at Territorial Headquarters numbered one hundred and sixty. The executive were all male. When it was known a woman was coming in as leader many considered it a 'nominal' appointment. She was only a front woman. The second in command would be left to deal with the tough stuff. Within a couple of weeks of her arrival it was evident Eva Burrows was quite able to make her own decisions, live with the consequences, and give anyone who shirked their own responsibility a sharp rap on the knuckles. This exceedingly capable lady was match for any man.

Apprehension about how she might be received in other denominations was equally short lived, despite a bomb scare when the Anglican archbishop was ordaining women as deacons in Melbourne. At an ecumenical service for peace in the Roman Catholic cathedral Eva was placed with all the other heads of churches, at the top near the altar. Grudging admiration soon gave way to total support. Australians have a strong sense of comradeship, a hang over from the pioneer days when sticking together could mean the difference between survival or an untimely end. Anyone who achieved anything for the good of a number of people was 'in'. Eva was achieving a great deal. It was in Australia that the full force of her leadership became apparent. As far as she was concerned the fact of her being a woman was almost irrelevant. The Army had a long history of women officers and leaders. She was simply doing the job she had been appointed to do. Those who expected her to jump on the 'women's lib bandwagon' were disappointed, married women in particular.

There is a long standing grievance in Army circles that for all their vaunted equality the men are still more equal than the women, and married women come well at the bottom of the pile. Some felt Eva's own achievements could only be an encouragement to women. Others felt her fairly conservative views did little to alleviate the situation. Any suggestion of affirmative action was anathema to her. Those in authority had to earn the right to be there. Just as she had done. She certainly wouldn't make appointments where a woman was put in a position of leadership just because she was a woman. If people didn't like that they must present a reasoned alternative.

At a staff conference in 1983 she warned, 'I don't want murmurs of assent now, and then critical comments and misgivings expressed in private discussion when the conference is over . . . Be prepared to offer opinions from the stance of reason, realism and experience. Then make concrete proposals of improvement.' The following year she told youth leaders she wanted to see a set of realistic, practical recommendations emerging from their meetings, 'Not vague, like last year'.

The lady at the top was beginning to jolt people out of the usual mould. Not everybody appreciated it. Some had to be quietly taken aside and advised to answer back. Not out of disrespect, but because Eva wanted them to be able to back their opinions; stand up for what they believed. Though there was no point presenting a case if they were not sure of their ground, and hadn't done their research thoroughly.

If argument failed, illustration could be a powerful weapon. On one occasion Eva was visiting the outback where she was introduced to the flying padre, who would be called in by radio to hold services or officiate at a wedding or burial. He offered to take Eva on a tour of the sheep and cattle stations in his area. As she climbed aboard the aircraft she remarked somewhat apprehensively that it appeared to be held together with little more than pieces of string. 'That's why I'm taking you,' came the quick reply.

Eva describes herself as an 'idealist without illusions'. She could certainly cut through other people's illusions and had no illusions about her own fallibility. She was just as prone to error as anyone else, the difference being she was not afraid to admit it or hold back from making decisions for fear of being wrong. When she was she didn't waste time agonising over her mistakes. She accepted responsibility, learned the necessary lessons and made mental note to make sure it did not happen again.

Her watchword was 'consultative leadership'. She liked to seek advice from those who had knowledge and expertise, discuss the possibilities and come to some form of consensus, with everyone hopefully agreeing with her own conclusions. If that was authoritarian – so be it. That was the Army style. They were all under authority, herself included. If she had any regrets they were all to do with the times when she had not taken more positive action.

The subject of divorce and remarriage caused her special heartache. Crises in her own family had left her in no doubt of the agony involved. Yet someone had to stand against the rising tide of family break up, and the devastation it left in its wake. The Salvation Army had seen too many casualties of divorce to take it lightly. She said: 'So many of the young people we are dealing with, who have severe emotional problems and great hang ups and grudges against society, are the children who come from broken homes.'

Concerned about various policies militating against family stability Eva wrote to the Prime Minister suggesting there should be a Minister for the Family. Her sister Margaret and Bramwell her husband are both involved in marriage counselling and enrichment. Whenever she had opportunity Eva took a firm stand against any slackening of principles, or pastoral care, especially when officers' marriages were involved. Those in positions of leadership somehow had to achieve a balance; strong principles against compassion, tradition against initiative, social work versus evangelical.

Eva gave them a superb example to follow. She was no remote demagogue pontificating from the mountain top. She could name all her top officers and their appointments. She could visualise their faces when their names came up for prayer or discussion, and empathise over the difficult decisions they sometimes had to face. The burden of pastoral care is always considerable – especially when you are responsible for one thousand officers and fifteen thousand Salvationists as Eva was in the Southern Territory. Not that she was likely to let it get her down. Her 'roots went deep into God's love' and His strength was far greater than her own.

'I read recently that it is in the "climate of faith" that there is great achievement and the impossible can happen,' said Commissioner Burrows lecturing her troops. 'May we have that faith which "laughs at impossibilities and cries it shall be done".'

It was. By the time she addressed her divisional commanders in 1986 the church growth programme was just beginning; they were commencing a new era in the Bridge programme, fresh developments in community care were under way, and the government was asking the Salvation Army to extend Employment 2000 to the older age group. When the Australia Day honours list was announced on January 26th, Commissioner Eva Burrows had been appointed an Officer in the General Division of the Order of Australia for her 'service to the community in Australia and humanity at large as a member of the Salvation Army'. For Eva it was the supreme confirmation of her acceptance in Australia.

'I wasn't proud for my own sake but it was lovely to know I'd done something in Australia, for Australia. It made up in a way for the fact that I'd deserted my country for a long, long time.' Was this to be the pinnacle of her career? The seal on all she had done so far? What was there left to achieve?

Her housekeeper had served many leaders in her long career in social services. One day in conversation with General Brown she commented that she had contact with most of the Generals from the time of General Higgins in the 1930s.

'And you'll be looking after the next one, won't you,' he

replied. The housekeeper pondered. So did Eva's family and Salvationists throughout the world. The current General, a Finn by the name of Jarl Wahlstrom, was retiring in July. A meeting of the High Council was convened for April. Eva already held one of the top positions in the Salvation Army world. All the leaders had tremendous respect for her. But there were other gifted people too. When the lots were cast there was no knowing in whose lap the responsibility might land.

CHAPTER TWENTY

The High Council was held at Sunbury Court, a Salvation Army conference and youth centre, fourteen miles south west of London. The forty six leading officers in the Salvation Army converged on the capital from twenty eight countries of the world. They were greeted by the Prime Minister, Margaret Thatcher, at a reception in Church House, Westminster, close to Westminster Abbey.

In his official welcome Commissioner Caughey Gauntlett described Margaret Thatcher as a woman who knew her own mind and had definite policies. 'Which we're not without in the Salvation Army,' he quipped.

Eva Burrows had been selected to respond to the Prime Minister's welcome. When she began to speak, wagging her finger reprovingly to emphasise certain points in true teacher fashion, the Prime Minister could have had little doubt to whom the Commissioner had been referring.

After the first flurry of welcomes and reunions at Sunbury Court everyone settled down to the serious matter of selecting the right person for the all-important job. Salvation Army style is very dependent on the leadership. The person at the top would be in charge for the next five years. A wrong decision could be disastrous. Electing a General was a solemn and sacred responsibility.

The peace of the spring countryside and the enduring qualities of the old building helped to create a prayerful atmosphere. The meetings and discussions were held round a long table in the panelled hall of the lecture room. The lengthy procedure has been compared to the Catholic

College of Cardinals electing a new Pope. It is the only election held by the Salvation Army and tends to follow a pattern which has proved successful over the years since the first High Council met in the year of Eva's birth.

There is no lobbying, no manifesto, little political manoeuvring, although obviously there is discussion behind the scenes about the various candidates. Eva had gifts and experience, but she was only fifty six. A new General was selected every five years. Why not wait? A candidate from the Third World had been nominated for the first time. He was a strong contender. If Eva stood at the next election she would still be a decade younger than some who had been appointed. On the other hand her talents were needed. It was a pity to pass them by.

Eva's name was put forward for nomination. She was back on her knees, querying her own reactions and motivation. Did she want to accept because it would be the crowning pinnacle of her service? To show that a woman could do it? Should she accept it? Others had got to that point and withdrawn. There would be no shame in that. The shame would come if she allowed her name to stand for all the wrong reasons or thought for one moment if she was elected it was by virtue of her own strength or ability. There was no voice from the skies, but the crystallisation of an awareness that it was right to stand. The outcome she was content to leave with God. If she was not appointed there was more than enough to occupy her in Australia. If she was . . . Well . . . He had not let her down so far.

Once the nominations had been accepted the pressure was on. Each of the seven candidates had to answer a series of questions covering subjects as varied as theology, style of management, Army principles, the internationalism of the Movement, their own personal health and homelife. Eva had no partner to consult about the prospect of such a prominent position but inevitably the subject of her health came under discussion. All she could do was be honest about the heart attack, but point out that in her recent two-yearly medical which all leaders had to undergo she had been informed she was now in good health.

She needed to be. The first hurdle was a half hour script to be prepared overnight outlining her views on the role of General. Eva was halfway through preparing the text of a speech on administration and organisation when she became uneasy. She was not one given to hearing voices, specific commands from the Almighty, but she knew something was wrong with the script. She looked at her watch. She was used to late nights but the hours were ticking on relentlessly. Had she time to start again from the beginning? She paused and prayed. It was as if the Lord was making her aware of the need to talk about the leadership of Jesus and following in his style. Once she had digested the idea the thoughts came thick and fast. Jesus, the pastor, prophet, priest. What better model could any leader have? It was not Eva Burrows saying 'See what I know. Vote for me', but the experience of more than a decade rooted in a firm foundation.

Delivering the speech was more daunting. Members were not allowed to respond or show support of any kind. An American delegate did once forget himself at a previous High Council and let rip with an enthuiastic 'Amen' but he hurriedly apologised. For the first time in her life Eva Burrows was talking to blank faces.

Slowly the secret ballots whittled down the candidates with the bottom one dropping off at each vote. No time limit was set but there had to be a two thirds majority on the final vote. After a week of deliberations and voting they reached the fourth ballot. There were only two names left. As one of the top three leaders in the world Eva was amongst the first to cast her vote. She resumed her seat and sat praying as others took their turn.

'Eva.'

Someone was whispering her name. She looked up, expecting to see the leader next to her signalling for her attention. His head was bowed in prayer. Everyone's mind was concentrated on the job in hand. Eva shook her head. The voice had been so clear. She thought of the story of the child Samuel running to his master when he heard a voice calling his name. Was God trying to tell her something?

'I don't know whether it's an experience the Lord allowed me, but it's the only time I've ever known anything like that.'

She waited quietly. One way or another God's will would soon be known. She had never been one to indulge in senseless fretting. The reverence her own family had felt towards the position of General was deeply ingrained. It was an awesome task. Whoever shouldered it was going to need all the support and prayers they could get. Prayer was a much more constructive use of her energy. As she prayed the words of an Army song came to her mind, adding to her sense of peace and confidence in God.

Though the future is veiled
Thou shalt not be afraid
For the peace of the Lord
On thy heart has been laid.

The final votes were cast. It was Friday May 2nd, 1986. 'We have a General,' the president announced. The lot had fallen to Eva. She was the youngest General since Bramwell Booth, and spiritual, inspirational and administrative head of one and a half million Salvationists and three million supporters in nearly ninety countries. As she stepped onto the platform Eva offered all she was and had to God. No matter how inadequate she might feel she knew if He had placed her in that position He would give sufficient strength – just as he had always done.

Once they knew a woman had been elected the world's press had a field day. The Anglicans had been debating whether a woman could be in charge of the handful of people in some local congregations for more than a decade. Now here was a woman head of a church worldwide. Most Salvationists wondered what all the fuss was about. In the Army men and women were both commissioned as officers. Theoretically they could rise through the ranks the same as men. They had had nominal equality for over a century. Eva Burrows was still only the second woman to hold supreme authority. The other was Evangeline Booth, daughter of the Founder, in the fateful years from 1934 to 1939, leading up to the Second World War. The parallels did not escape notice.

Eva shrugged the comparisons aside. Evangeline had been in her seventies when she took office; it had almost been an anti-climax after her dramatic years as head of the Army in Canada and America. She was known for her eloquence and showmanship. Eva belonged to a different era. Whatever similarities 'Fighting Mac' may have seen in their personalities Eva had no intention of becoming a carbon copy. She believed communication in the 1980s depended on being able to speak the language of the common people rather than the kind of oratory for which Evangeline was famed. If she became known as a 'people's General' that would suit her fine. It was where she belonged. She did not come from a famous Salvation Army family. She was the eighth child of two dedicated but ordinary Australian officers. If anyone was going to get the Salvation Army back to its origins it would be Eva Burrows. She had not forgotten her roots even if she had suddenly found herself sitting on the top branch.

The full impact of events hardly had time to register as the press clamoured for attention. A woman leader made good headlines. 'Don't call this General Sir'; 'The General is a Lady'; 'Woman heads the Army'. Could she do an interview for radio, television, yet another newspaper? How about a few words on video? It wouldn't take a minute. Just a short message for Salvationists around the world who would want to know what the next five years had in store for them. There was no time for preparation. Eva was already on her way to the airport. She arrowed a quick prayer as they posed her in front of a portrait of William Booth. As a teacher she was used to having her facts at her finger tips, a logical lesson plan; not talking off the top of her head. Sermons and greetings were always prepared in advance. How could she address the vast audience a video could attract almost at the drop of a hat?

'Lord . . . the right words . . . please.' Her head was in a whirl. There was so much to absorb. The interviews, congratulations, the essential briefing sessions with the retiring General. When she arrived back at Tullamarine airport, Melbourne, after the long twenty eight hour journey from England it was like the arrival of Miss World. Cameras flashed, bands played, flags waved. There was another long session with the press. Eva could hardly keep her eyes open. If this was a foretaste of what was to come there was no question of Eva Burrows trusting in her own strength. She was going to be permanently in that place where we all function best if we would only admit it. Dependent on the One who is the source of all strength.

Sunday May 11th was Mother's Day. Family and friends gathered to congratulate Eva. Her brothers and sisters were 'exultant'. All that their mother had dreamed of had been achieved. As long as Eva was in leadership their parents memory would never die. Everywhere she went they were told 'I see your mother in the pulpit', or 'She has her father's capability at decision making'.

Their happiness was completed when Margaret, Bramwell and their daughter Claire accompanied Eva when she received her 'Order of Australia' award at Government House. It was a fitting send off from her homeland. So was the opening of the hostel of the homeless which had taken so many hours of her time and energy. She had kept her promise. It was one of the last things she did before leaving Australia.

Messages of congratulation and farewell continued to pour in from all quarters of the globe. One read simply 'There has been a lot of water and many bridges to cross since the journey of the *Otranto'* in 1950. Then Eva had set sail for London as an unknown young woman in a hand-sewn outfit. Now she was head of an international organisation and her photograph was on papers and newscreens throughout the world.

At the High Council it would have been normal procedure to ask if a wife was prepared to share the burden of responsibility if her husband was elected General. No one thought to ask Eva how she would cope as a single woman. Fortunately she had her own support networks. They swung into action. Margaret and Mrs Groves did all they could to smooth the transition back to England. A Major Ian Southwell from the theological college in Australia wrote a reasoned article which was published in Army journals for the sake of any critics who doubted whether a woman could, or should, assume leadership. Eva would have been quite capable of writing in her own defence but it seemed more appropriate coming from a man. Major Southwell argued from Scripture and the early church as the Army 'mother', Catherine Booth, had done when she fought the self same battles at the end of the previous century.

'If there is in Jesus Christ "neither male nor female" . . . who shall dare thrust woman out of the church's operations or presume to put any candle which God has lighted under a bushel? Why should the swaddling bands of blind custom . . . be again wrapped round the female disciples of the Lord?' wrote the indignant Catherine in one of her love letters to William.

The world would certainly have been a lot darker if women had not been allowed to play their part in the development of the movement. The first women evangelists were appointed in 1875. Women's right to be commissioned was written into the Army constitution. An article illustrating the liberation of women by Jesus appeared in the pages of *War Cry* nearly one hundred years ago. Generations of women doctors, social workers, teachers and ministers have marched in the Army's ranks, proving the accuracy of William Booth's words 'Some of my best men are women'.

Eva considered her own mother's ministry to be one of the 'most effective' she had known and saw no reason why women should not use the talents God had given them to the full. She was not an extreme feminist but she stood by the gospel principle that all were of equal value in God's sight, as Jesus had shown in his attitudes and teaching. Anglican women who were finding the long haul towards women's ministry frustrating should not be impatient. It would come more by evolution than revolution.

Those who had seen the heartbreak that failure to acknowledge the wife's contribution could cause within their own ranks remained unconvinced.

'If Catherine Booth had believed that, Eva Burrows would not be General of the Salvation Army,' remarked one of her women officers who had shared the distress of a number of talented women whose names were not even mentioned when their husbands received a new posting. It is certainly difficult to imagine Eva content with a 'back up' role or taking too happily to what has traditionally been seen as 'women's jobs' for any length of time. When she was appointed to social services many saw it as a sideways move, and felt Eva would not have appreciated being stuck with the 'woman' tag for the rest of her service. Although she considers marriage a 'beautiful gift' and the welfare of children during their early years of prime importance she is first to admit that if she was married balancing the role of mother and minister of the gospel 'would create a great deal of tension'. She certainly could not have been General if she had married. There is only one General and a wife cannot hold a position superior to her husband. Although married women may still feel grievance, Eva obviously is aware of the problems and is seeking to redress the balance as far as appointments are concerned though the day when 'The General and Mr Whoever' are announced could still be little more than cause for wry amusement in Army kitchens.

Lord Thurso, who had shared not only Eva's spectacles but many of her insights, feared when she was elected General that the media would try to typecast her as a woman. He felt she had all the attributes needed to command the Army; enthusiasm, faith, vision and courage.

He hoped 'the fact of being a woman never obscures her qualities or hides from view the work which she is doing'.

If the opinions of those who had worked with her in Africa, Great Britain, Sri Lanka, Australia, were anything to go by he had no cause for concern. The attributes they listed included adaptability, an excellent brain, ability to assimilate facts, assess a situation, act accordingly and win people's confidence. At her welcome to International Headquarters when she took up her post in July she was described as the 'kind of leader people love to follow'. All the emphasis was on qualities of leadership. The fact that she was a woman hardly came into consideration apart from a certain anxiety about whether the men would be able to stand the pace. A male colleague who had worked with her in Australia summed up the feeling. He was delighted when he heard she had been elected General but 'was sure he would live to regret it'.

Not that anyone feared an era of petticoat government. Far from it. The fears were more to do with the tightening up of standards everyone sensed would inevitably follow in the wake of Eva's own high expectations. *The Times* commented on Eva's qualities of self discipline and single mindedness. One of her staff put it more simply: 'She knows what she wants and sets out to get it.'

Eva would probably take issue with that verdict. She talks always of commitment rather than career. Her avowed aim is 'to please God'. She insists she has always sought to give of her best in each situation God has placed her. She has never believed in 'looking over her shoulder' to see who was competing in the leadership stakes. Ambition and aggression were masculine qualities. She wanted to lead 'as a woman'. Women were equal but different. She agreed with Catherine Booth. They should complement rather than compete with the men. She would not use 'feminine wiles' but women had their own skills to bring to the task. She believed in disarming rather than confrontation. Those who had clashed with her at various times must have smiled wryly when they heard that. In a conflict situation it was not usually Eva who retired at the first round.

The last chapter of Proverbs lists the qualities of a 'good woman'. An Australian newspaper, *The Age* ran a review of Eva's characteristics. Charming, tough, persuasive, verging on the workaholic, no nonsense type, not bossy. The wholeness her sister Margaret had sensed after Eva made her decision to follow Christ had matured with the years but was still as obvious. She had a good balance of masculine and feminine. She had a ready grasp of concepts, but that did not blind her to the needs of people.

The Army had definitely found themselves a good woman though whether the subject of women's ministry is really the 'minor issue' she believes it to be is open to debate. Statements such as 'The Christian gospel is much too important to spend time discussing who is qualified to minister. The Church needs every man and woman available to spread the gospel' must have been greeted with an equal mixture of Hallelujahs and groans of despair.

CHAPTER TWENTY ONE

Eva had no doubt where her priorities lay. Almost before the staff at IHQ had time to digest the fact that a new General was 'in control' she was laying down an 'Agenda for the Future' with evangelism head of the list. 'We are forever saying "Evangelism is our supreme purpose",' she challenged. 'Do we live up to that?'

Second in line came spiritual renewal. Wasn't that rather putting the cart before the horse? It was all very well attracting people into the movement. What would they find when they got there? Living water or a stagnant pool?

Eva sighs. The idealist is under no illusions about the inbreeding and infighting that can take place in some corps, the dangers of second and third generation Salvationism or the fact that corps in suburbia still flourish while they are thin on the ground in the downtown areas closest to the Founder's heart. Even harder to digest is the lack of teaching which has left soldiers 'weakened by spiritual malnutrition' and in 'no fit state' to share their faith. The light of battle glints in her eye. She squares her shoulders. When she is on the platform there will be no mistaking the call, no mismatch of beliefs with behaviour. What Salvationists say and sing on a Sunday should be lived out in the office, or on the factory floor, the rest of the week.

In her tour of welcome during her first few months in office General Burrows missed no opportunity of challenging her troops. People needed to 'find again the spiritual dimension in a world that has become increasingly secular'. There was no room for defeatism, bewailing the problems. Jesus had spelt it out clearly enough. They were to go out into the world. Not sit waiting for people to come to them when there were so many other distractions. The Salvation Army has always had a sense of compulsion about the need 'to win souls'. Now they must grope for a 'new expression of evangelism'.

In the United States and in Australia church growth principles were getting things moving. Eva had seen it in action. She supported the principles wholeheartedly; the use of the laity, small groups, personal witness. Evangelism was not just the prerogative of the officer. Or the General. Every soldier was an evangelist, a disciple maker. As she was driving to Sunbury for the High Council Eva had noticed a poster proclaiming 'Go for growth'. That would be her aim, and the aim of her followers, if she could mobilise them once more into an effective fighting force. Some of the troops were ready and waiting. All they needed was a clear trumpet call, a positive lead.

Although numbers indicated that the Army in Britain and Europe was winding down there were pockets open to change and renewal which had been given a 'second wind' as the Holy Spirit blew through the churches. Salvationists are not a 'speaking in tongues' people. Like the apostle Paul, Eva considers tongues a 'lesser gift', but she has no hesitation in encouraging her followers to 'a greater awareness of the Holy Spirit – a personal Pentecost'. Her own walk with God has been a constant realignment with God's purposes and dependence on him. The Salvation Army have always considered themselves charismatic. In Africa and many parts of the Third World the younger churches are still live with the 'blood and fire' of the early days.

'We believe the Salvation Army got its identity and style and everything from the guidance of the Holy Spirit. It wasn't something we sat down and planned. He gave it to us,' says Eva.

William Booth had found himself getting bogged down

in committees. The concept of an Army had instant appeal. Armies got things moving. Their very discipline and structure made sure of that. The Salvation Army is always being praised for being first on the site in an emergency. The symbolism goes right back to New Testament teaching; the soldier equipped for battle, though the war the Army pursues is against suffering and evil. In 1986 the Salvation Army was nominated for the Nobel Peace Prize for the second time. Far from being a disadvantage the discipline could be an attraction, a stability in a world where freedom too often means doing your own thing regardless of who gets hurt in the process.

Not many churches demand so much of their young people in terms of commitment and disciplined lifestyle yet Salvationist youth workers believe many are 'fed up with fripperies', disillusioned with the violence and lowering of standards they see in the world around them. Whereas five, ten years ago youngsters would have sniggered at any suggestion of Bible study, now 'you could hear a pin drop' in study sessions. The young Salvationists highlighted in Army publications have a 'wholesomeness' about them it would be difficult to find in a secular journal. They are not so far removed from the Eva Burrows of forty years ago, newly converted and full of zeal. Neither are the rebels. Eva's own rebellion helps her appreciate the traumas teenagers face in their search for identity and a faith that is real. She is still young at heart and the years spent working in Africa have given her great faith in young people. Wherever she goes she notes particularly what the young have to say. She takes an interest in their concerns.

'She's a visionary lady. She feels the vibes. She moves round the world and she's aware of something happening in our young people. She's got her finger on the button.'

She's also well aware of the Army's limitations, especially where young people's work is concerned. A fair proportion of corps have no worker responsible for young people and one of the first things she notices when she visits a centre is how far the young people are involved. 'If we don't encourage them, train them, use them, then we are doing a great dis-service to the Army,' she warns. The bowed heads and shamed faces tell her the diagnosis is correct.

In its early days the Army was a young people's movement. Revival in Wales was started by a seventeen-year-old. A girl a year younger helped found the Army in America. The 'Hallelujah lasses', young girl officers, were one of the early attractions. Eva Burrows was preaching a sermon and leading the youth work before she was out of her teens. She believes in continuing the tradition. To her mind someone of a similar age will have far more impact on young people than one whose hair shows they are the wrong side of forty, however young at heart they still feel.

'I admire the devil,' said one young Salvationist introducing a talk. Everyone sat bolt upright. Including Eva. 'I thought "Good on you, mate. You've got their attention".'

She believes that in a visually orientated age anything that will 'get their fingers out of their ears' is worth noting. Preaching must be more than pleasantries and social justice exposes. 'It should be biblically based but relevant to the situation in which people live. There's still a place for it in a service but we should use every opportunity to use the modern media; drama, choreography, music, visuals, illustrations.'

Her own style is lively, conversational, containing a profusion of illustrations but presenting the central truth seriously. William Booth set the standard. Ella Burrows showed the way. Eva was a ready student. As a teacher she knows communication is all important. Lose the attention of your listeners and you might as well give up on the spot. If your mind does not believe what your lips are saying you become as a sounding gong or tinkling cymbal. All the bands in the world are of no avail.

Not that she is anti-band. The battles she fought in Scotland show she will fight to the last breath to keep the Army's right to play and witness on the streets. What she does question is the whens and wherefores. If soldiers are serious about evangelism, spreading the good news, do they need to review the times and places of their open air witness? After service rather than before when people are still in bed? The shopping mall on Saturday in preference to an empty Sunday morning street? She knows it will inconvenience people, put their schedule out but has her answer at the ready. 'That's what being a soldier means.'

In no way does she support retreat into the citadel or preserving the status quo with a 'this is how we've always done it' philosophy. Hymn sandwiches are out. Rhythm groups, eye-catching literature, drama, the use of the media, anything that conveys the gospel in 'contemporary and culturally relevant terms' requires serious consideration. Not to be 'gimmicky' but to get across the message.

When someone expressed disapproval at the singing of religious words to a secular tune William Booth responded 'Why should the devil have all the best tunes?' A hundred years later opinions are still divided on whether contemporary music is a marvellous tool for communication or an instrument the devil is welcome to keep. Just as they are about assimilating modern songs and choruses with a proven track record across the denominational spectrum, or sticking to Army music that some of the younger generation feel has 'become frozen and traditionalised in that early style'.

The person at the top has a delicate path to tread. On one side the vested interests of bands, musicians and publishing houses. On the other the need to give 'modern young Salvationists modern tools to win the war against Satan's kingdom.'

Army periodicals have already come in for an overhaul. The magazine *War Cry* with its long history and wide distribution came in for a re-style in 1986. The result is a magazine much more geared to the concerns of secular readers with a good blend of interesting articles, news, views, reviews and humour.

Most of the territories now have a Communications

Department, and the use and production of videos is growing in importance. Young officers in America and Australia where each town may have its own radio or TV station are trained in the use of modern media. In Britain many still fight shy of the press despite the recent spate of good publicity with soup runs and sleeping bags for the homeless, their work in helping distribute part of the EEC butter mountain to the poor and elderly, and their sparkling lady General. So far she has outcharmed Terry Wogan, was perfectly 'at home' with Cliff Michelmore and was complimented for being 'better than all the film stars' on one of her numerous appearances on radio.

'I'm certainly not afraid of the media. I use every opportunity. If I can get time on TV even if it pushes me under the ground to prepare I'll take it. I wish we had more.'

Not that Eva aspires to join the ranks of the American TV evangelists but she is a teacher, a communicator, and it shows. She appreciates the size of the audience and the immediate one-to-one contact.

'I don't consider I'm a quick thinker. All I do is talk to the interviewer when I'm on television. I forget all about the apparatus.' The viewers don't forget her so easily. Mention Eva Burrows, the lively Australian leader of the Salvation Army, and most people remember seeing her on 'the telly'.

In a world geared to image the Army has frequently been criticised for being fuddy-duddy, and out of step with the age. Eva will have none of it. To her mind meetings are alive and attractive. The uniform gets you noticed. An officer in mufti walking through a crowded railway station is no different to anyone else. The girl in the navy blue bonnet might know where you could get a bed for the night, or give you a phone card to call home and tell them you are safe.

A Salvation Army officer was practising for an ecumenical service in Westminster Abbey. She was standing with several other clergymen discussing where everyone should stand. One of the Abbey guides headed towards them.

'There's a man outside who needs some help,' he said, addressing the Salvationist and ignoring the other clerics. 'Could you come?' In the 'backs to the wall' situation which the Western church now faces Eva delights to see some of the barriers coming down and a new emphasis on co-operation rather than confrontation. When she returned to Sri Lanka in 1987 she felt a 'great surge of love' from the other churches.

'They welcomed me back as a sister in Christ. I was invited to preach in the cathedral on Christian Unity Sunday. All the church leaders were there, including the RC archbishop and his bishops.'

The story is repeated wherever she travels. Church leaders are now getting together to discuss the many causes for concern they share; poverty, unemployment, apartheid, the problems of the inner city. Salvationists are often 'happily involved at grass roots' if there is a clearly defined purpose. Practical rather than political. Mission more than discussion. 'If it's dialogue that's just open ended we tend to drop off. We don't see the point.'

Eva has worshipped with many different denominations over the years and realises that not everyone appreciates the Army's style. In no way does she see the Army as right and everyone else out of step. There is room for all, and the Salvation Army has a place alongside others and a responsibility to fulfil the purpose for their existence. She regrets that so often outsiders think of the Army purely as a social agency. To her they are very much part of the body of Christ. The hands maybe?

'You can only show a caring God by action,' she insists. 'People are far more impressed by what you do than by what you say. It's an indictment of us all when we don't live up to our faith.'

CHAPTER TWENTY TWO

As head of the Salvation Army General Eva Burrows is responsible for food distribution centres, occupational centres, children's homes, hostels, hospitals and clinics in eighty-nine different countries. The number of buildings run into hundreds. The people helped into millions.

From childhood she has learnt that service and spiritual growth are two strands of the same theme. Jesus himself warned would be followers of the dangers of calling him Lord but ignoring the needs of the people around them. Working as they often do in the downtown deprived areas generations of Salvationists have found it almost impossible not to be involved.

When questioned about motivation Eva is vehement that the social work is 'not a hook to angle souls – it grows out of our compassion and love'. The two are inseparable. A religious movement without any social dimension becomes little more than a back street mission. A social agency with no spiritual work is only one of a number of professional and voluntary agencies. The fact they have both gives the Salvation Army its character and identity. 'If you can get at the root of people's problems . . . and get their spiritual lives right then they can cope with the big distresses of life – go through them – rather than be crushed under them.'

The few months in social services gave Eva a good grounding in the fallibility of human nature, and the various aspects of the work. When she visits institutions on her trips round the world she does not just see a group; the elderly, handicapped, homeless, but individuals who are valuable to God. A trip along the Thames embankment taking sleeping bags and soup to people sleeping on the streets in sub-zero temperatures is not an ordeal but an opportunity. She wishes there was time for more. One of the biggest drawbacks of holding a top administrative post is being removed from the people you are aiming to serve. When one of the 'clients' at a rehabilitation centre in America presented her with a charcoal sketch of herself Eva's instinctive reaction was to give him a hug. 'She kissed the likes of me,' he said wonderingly to his mates. 'She shows the light of Christ.'

Not all Salvationists share her natural warmth or distinct 'bias to the poor' but she makes sure they are continually being called to be open, available and aware of the needs of their area. Social work does not stop when the doors close on the last applicant to the big hostels in the inner city. Playgroups, lunch clubs, keep fit, unemployment initiatives, have all helped break down the barriers and restore corps where the church rightfully belongs: back in the community. Publications like the *War Cry* deal with subjects such as debt, AIDS, sexual abuse of children, relationships, in a realistic 'Here's what you can do about it' format. A new social and moral issues group keeps the General informed and alert. She is not only aware of areas where the church should be speaking with authority but, as in Australia, making sure she has adequate ammunition before she declares war.

A series of letters and documents to government bodies have expressed Army concern on such matters as the extension of licensing hours, religious education and various matters affecting the family. She agrees the Army should have no party political bias but looks as though she may have as much trouble as her Master trying not to get involved in matters which concern people. 'I think we should feel strongly about social injustice . . . If "political" means speaking out on issues such as prostitution or abortion, poverty and homelessness, if speaking out to quicken the conscience of the government on the needs of the people is political then I'm political. I'm not just protesting for protesting's sake - I want to get something done.'

There is certainly plenty to keep her occupied. William Booth's 'cab horse charter' set out to ensure the basic right of every individual to the three requisites of food, shelter and work which were considered the norm for London cab horses if not the lower classes at the turn of the last century. As we head towards the twenty first century a trip on the Docklands light railway only minutes walk from International Headquarters shows just how extreme the contrasts between rich and poor still are, even in the affluent West. Doesn't such a thought drive Eva to despair? Her answer is unequivocal.

'Yes. I look at people homeless and sad as I did the night I went round and saw them all sleeping rough, or the unemployed and I just say "What can you do?" "Where can you begin?" That's when your positive side comes in and you do what you can. And pray that together with all the others who are working in this field we will make inroads on the tragedy.'

For the alcoholic it probably means making sure he has adequate health care, counselling, spiritual teaching. Homeless people may be helped by converting buildings which no longer serve their original purpose into emergency accommodation. Local attempts to ease the nightmare of unemployment need co-ordination, and expert advice on finance and resources. The appointment of a lay consultant on unemployment in 1987 was a new initiative. So was the publication of a practical booklet for relatives and friends of AIDS patients. With so many casualties of modern society no one agency or organisation can handle all the human need of a population. The Army is still needed and frequently called on for assistance. Counselling relatives waiting for news when the ferry capsized at Zeebrugge, serving refreshments to the firemen at King's Cross underground fire, caring for the babies of heroin addicts, converting a former leper colony in Zambia into an AIDS unit.

The needs of the Western world may be considerable. The Army is an international organisation. Two-thirds of its membership live in the Third World. There the problems can be overwhelming. What can even an activist like Eva Burrows do against such odds?

Large-scale disasters like the terrible famines in Ethiopia are obviously beyond their scope, but wherever the Army is operational there is work for them to do. Agricultural programmes in Africa, vocational training for handicapped people in India, kindergartens in Hong Kong. During a visit to the Far East Eva visited a kindergarten in the heart of the old walled city where the buildings are piled one on top of the other with no proper streets, no drainage, no sanitation. In the middle of it all a door opened and there were 'these gorgeous little Chinese children - being taught by very well trained Chinese girls.'

The long-term development programmes always have the most enduring benefits but emergency aid still remains vital in many areas. Since Eva has been General there have been floods in Brazil and Bangladesh, drought in Southern Africa, an earthquake in Salvador, refugees on the borders of Mozambique. From her experience in Africa and the hurricane in Sri Lanka Eva knows that those commissioned to preach the gospel, heal the sick, feed the poor cannot turn their back on the hungry and homeless.

'I understand the people who say don't give them a fish, give them a hook and teach them how to fish. We've got plenty of those kind of programmes. But - as a Christian - if I see a man who's hungry I'll feed him. When you see the starving as we did in Ethiopia - all those bloated bellies and pleading eyes - do you think Jesus Christ could turn them away? I'd like those people who say you can't feed the hungry bellies - you're just using up resources - to stand in front of those queues and try saying, "Sorry. No food. Go away and die".'

At Usher the 'Oxfarm' kitchen kept the village children from starvation. Pupils who had a long walk to school with nothing in their stomachs were always given breakfast before the day's work began. There is no lack of ideas to meet the needs. The problems are always to do with money.

In the autumn of 1987 Eva visited the Caribbean where her great-grandfather went to work when William Booth was ten years old. The plane flew over the islands strung out like pearls in a necklace. At the grand parade in Jamaica the flags of sixteen nations were in the march. She went to the blind school. The braille library was the best in Jamaica, yet the government was having to cut the subsidy. Down town they found a similar story. A centre with a feeding programme for old people, a clinic, and a day nursery but never enough cash.

'The tears didn't roll down my cheeks but they were in my heart. Such need. Such poverty. You just feel you want to have the resources to expand the work. So many of the developing countries are log jammed economically. They haven't got enough funds. That's when I feel so proud of our officers who work such long hours without any hope of personal reward.'

And so distressed by a world where a painting by Van Gogh can sell for an amount which would feed millions of people world-wide. A copy might hang on her wall. The vibrancy and colour give as much pleasure every time she passes as it did all those years ago at Howard. The price still seems a travesty when people have to queue for a bowl of sazda or rice for their daily meal. The love of money may be the root of all evil. The lack of it comes a close second in Salvation Army circles. Despite the gifts of Salvationists, and government and international aid there is still never enough to go round. We may live in a 'global village' where we see tragedies as they happen on the screen in the corner of every living room. That doesn't prevent us putting up the barriers which say 'Enough', 'No more,' 'Me first.'

As she travels round the world Eva sees increasing signs of people entrenching themselves behind national barriers. 'Nationalism can be very narrow, self focusing, selfish, self centred. The global village sounds nice but I don't see all that much evidence of the preparedness to sacrifice for the sake of others that we do in a family.'

Nobody prepared to go to the wash tub ? Sell home made preserves? Sit up till midnight making a new dress? Give one-tenth of their income, as is now being suggested in Salvation Army circles? Eva has strong feelings on the matter. The eighth child from a poor Salvation Army family in the years of the Depression knows what she is talking about when it comes to sharing resources. She firmly resists any suggestion that the Army should become a federation rather than a family, however diverse the nations and cultures that contribute to it. To her the gospel crosses every culture. Her years at the ICO taught her that a Salvationist from India frequently has more in common with a Salvationist from Australia than two non-Salvationist Australians .

Army papers and magazines certainly have an international flavour. News of people, projects, corps, centenaries, celebrations, sorrows, span the globe. Attempts at 'cross pollination' include a choir from Soweto taking part in celebrations in Scotland, a family from India going to work in Guyana, an officer from Singapore developing work among the boat people in Melbourne, and several Koreans working in the USA.

The Salvation Army may have been slow starting but the 'buzz word' in America is definitely 'ethnic ministries.' There is a great need for pastors and evangelists to work amongst their own people in the various ethnic groups in the big cities, or for the 'special' brand of person who will be prepared to learn the language and identify with the people of a particular area. In other words, a few Eva Burrows in embryo.

Her love for Africa and the people of the Third World is obviously deep and genuine. A return visit to Zimbabwe gave her great joy. The love, the enthusiasm, the bright faces, the best march she has witnessed since becoming General. The return of so many words of Shona, which she hasn't spoken for nearly two decades. Reunions with past pupils who are now in their forties and fifties and holding responsible positions in business, politics and education. A meeting with the Prime Minister.

Not that it was without sadness. The two British girls who had died at Usher were not the only casualties of the years of unrest. She heard of many other deaths, including those of former colleagues whose Christ-like spirit will live on in the hearts of those who remember them. The problems still are many, but Eva takes an optimistic view.

'As a missionary I must take the blame that we changed the African's life so much. I remember reading in a book once that the sounds that have changed the face of Africa are the church bell and the jingle of coins in the pocket. We must take responsibility, and see that we direct that change into ways and opportunities for the Africans, no matter what the problems. I believe the African at heart wants the best for his country and in Zimbabwe where so many of the political leaders have had a good Christian education I'm positive and hopeful for the future.'

As 'international inspirer of the troops' her first few months in office have taken her to India, Hong Kong, the Philippines, Zimbabwe, Zambia, Jamaica, Sweden, Finland, the Netherlands, Italy and America. Her diary reads like an international airline schedule with a few stops for administration in between. So extensive is her itinerary she was recently given VIP status at Heathrow airport; an honour granted to only three other church leaders: the Chief Rabbi, the Archbishop of Westminster, and the Moderator of the Free Church of Scotland.

Centenaries, conferences, special celebrations all demand the presence of the General, and have given her a bird's eye view of the world. That computer memory is more useful than ever when it comes to retaining facts about people, places, and current issues of national and international importance. 'I read a great deal. We are fed all the time with reports from the countries of the world. I'm a quick reader. I can browse through a report, see the key points and summarise them.' Developments in Sri Lanka have given her special cause for concern recently. Her visit in 1987 was greeted with elephants, firecrackers and traditional instruments and dances. She was able to open a childcare centre and home for the handicapped in the buildings where she had been involved in planning and development during her time as Territorial Commander. A Peace Year log book signed by people from every corps and institution affirmed the desire of Salvationists to be active peacemakers. Before the end of the year children in one of the Salvation Army homes in Jaffna were sheltering in trenches while the bullets whizzed overhead. They could not get out. They had nowhere else to go.

'It's dreadfully sad to think of the situation as it is now,' said Eva, 'There are plenty of people in Sri Lanka, Tamils and Singalese, who really want there to be peace in the land. I would feel that the Christian church does have a lot to say in that situation because love is really the binding force for us.'

So that the burden does not become too great the Territorial Commanders and international secretaries shoulder many of the day-to-day responsibilities and act as go betweens, advising on situations and feelings in their section of the world and feeding back information from IHQ. Along with several of her predecessors Eva sees the urgent need for more indigenous leadership. All too often the Salvation Army, along with other Christian denominations, has been seen as a 'white man's church'. In the Caribbean the leadership was almost totally white until the last twenty years. It is changing but the image remains. Eva would like to see radical changes in this direction. 'Reinforcement', people becoming redundant; national officers trained for national leadership; national theologians prepared to answer some of the questions that are being asked at all levels; more international leadership at international headquarters.

'It is a long term process,' explains one of the national

leaders now working in London. 'But if the person at the top begins to express that kind of view it goes a long way towards changing attitudes. If she's convinced that people in the Third World have something to offer it goes a long way to convincing people.'

Despite a slow start it is already beginning to happen in relation to women. The General has said it is time to assess whether proper use is being made of both single and married women officers. People are beginning to take the point, and are almost 'falling over one another to appoint women'.

In the Third World they have a particularly significant part to play. When Eva was in Zimbabwe the Home League members would often teach the mothers the skills that their children were learning at school, in order to bridge the gap between the elders and their educated youngsters. That has been extended. Many of the Home leagues are becoming teaching centres for health programmes, training people in basic health and lifeskills.

All the time Eva and senior officers are on the look out for ability and potential. Others who will continue the tasks of healing, preaching, teaching, administration. The possibility of a Third World General may not be too far over the horizon. There are many gifted people around. Often all they lack is international experience, an opportunity to discover the 'nuances of culture' which came as such a shock to the brash Australian moving from Africa to the affluent West. Time to adjust from situations where they have oversight of millions of souls to one where millions of dollars can too easily take precedence. An awareness on the part of their colleagues of the 'hidden biases' which are in all of us, and the courage to face up to them.

As head of an international organisation Eva Burrows is constantly in contact with people of other cultures, other religions, other political persuasions. They must all be treated with respect, greeted as those who are of equal worth in God's sight. There is an immediate rapport with all who bear heavy burdens of state. A trip to the White House meant special prayer for President Reagan who admitted that like Abraham Lincoln there were many times when he was forced to his knees in prayer for there was 'no other place to go'.

All this requires great sensitivity. Negotiating complex political and cultural situations can feel like walking a minefield. The Army holds firm to its original policy of dealing with people, regardless of their politics. Individual Salvationists have as much freedom as anyone to express their personal opinions and a lay Salvationist is a member of Parliament in Britain at the moment. As representatives of the movement they have to be more circumspect. Experience has shown that 'If you get politically involved you get tossed out of a country and what can you do then?'

There was a highly charged political situation in the Caribbean during a serious rice shortage. A shipment of rice was sitting on the quayside. The party in power would not give clearance for its distribution in case the opposition used it as a political weapon. In the end it was decided to allow the Salvation Army to take charge because they were the only organisation which would not use it politically. In South Africa a new College has recently opened where black, white and coloured students are working and studying together.

Given her background it is not really surprising that in December 1986 General Eva Burrows issued a strong statement on apartheid although it came as a shock to some Salvationists. 'There have been people who have not agreed with that. Who felt that was a political statement and the Salvation Army was supposed to be non-political. I've had letters. I'd say apartheid is not just a political policy. It really is a philosophy of life. Our involvement is with people, black, white or coloured, whatever the political philosophy of that country.' Anything other than that is anathema to a 'closely knit international Christian movement – totally opposed to discrimination on racial, social or any other grounds.'

Political or not, that is one issue on which an international leader who has spent seventeen of the happiest years of her life working with black people is not going to be moved.

CHAPTER TWENTY THREE

Much of the first two years of Eva Burrows' term of office has been taken up with an almost non-stop welcome tour. 'Winning friends and influencing people,' joked one member of her staff. Wherever she has gone she has spoken to packed houses and felt a great surge of affection from the people.

'She says people nourish her, and it's true. She'll be absolutely flaked out then people appear and suddenly she's alive. We are nearly always last away from any meeting we go to. I've said to her more than once "You don't have to wait until the last person has gone before you go," but while there's anybody to speak with her she'll stay.'

Lords and ladies flock to any meeting she attends in Scotland. The people of Australia were thrilled when she was appointed General, and gave her a special welcome when she returned during their bicentenary year. In Sri Lanka the phone never stopped ringing. Everybody wanted to speak to her. Bishops, ministers, the ordinary people. America was a different proposition. It was the one continent she had never really worked in, but which plays such a large part in the Army world. Would they accept her? Could she reach their wavelength? She need not have worried. 'She went over like a bomb.'

At her welcome to International Headquarters on her first official day as General her second in command in Australia summarised the reasons for her popularity. 'She has the common touch and a royal air . . . I have seen her in the presence of the governor, the premier, business men, alcoholics, abused mothers and children, the unemployed. No difference to her. They were all sheep for whom the shepherd died.'

Eva describes herself as a 'people person'. If there is a conflict between administration and people, people invariably win. She will catch up with the administration later - when everyone else is in bed.

A few may still have reservations about her style, though they cannot help but admire the way she commands the platform. Other Generals have been gifted but not nearly so imposing. As a preacher she has 'a way with words,' which can be almost hypnotic. If her talents were not fully given to God she could be on very dangerous territory. She speaks with authority and expects people to listen. The 'born teacher' is still very much in evidence. There will be no slouching in the back row or mumbling of words while General Burrows is leading the singing. She paces backwards and forwards, arms waving, pouring her heart and soul into the proceedings. At the end not a hair is out of place. She looks as immaculate as she did when she stepped into the foyer of her block of flats to wait for her car that morning. Maybe a slight adjustment to the headgear, a smoothing of the navy skirt, a glance into the glass panels of the bookcase to check that all is in order, and she is ready for the next task.

'We take our pleasures seriously,' she jokes after preaching at three two-hour sessions in Westminster Central Hall in one day. She is already putting observations on tape, to refresh her memory when it comes to planning the meetings for 1989.

Her energy is formidable but she is not forbidding. She wants to know your impressions, even though she might not agree with them. Traditionally Salvationists have held the post of General in some awe as her own family did. That would be the last thing Eva Burrows would wish. On an interview with Terry Wogan on BBC television she said, 'I'm not stuffy. We like to think that our leaders are not distant from people but are really very friendly. Like you are, Terry. You'd make a good Salvationist.'

In a journey from the airport to the hotel it would be quite natural for her to start up a conversation with the taxi driver. It is part of the Australian friendliness. There you would sit in the front seat next to the driver. None of this nonsense about sliding panels, impersonal contact.

'She only needs to meet people once and she knows all about them. She recognises them. Puts them in the right pigeon holes.'

When she was elected General she received a telephone call from her former teacher, Mr Adsett, one of her 'shining people'. She recognised his voice immediately, after nearly fifty years. Mention a place, a person she can give you an instant rundown. Droitwich ? 'They came to see me from there. On a sponsored walk. They bought me a book of pictures the children had done. They have a new citadel. Very alive.'

It is not just in Britain. Wherever she goes round the world she recognises and remembers people. Students from thirty years ago in Zimbabwe. The older women she knew in the villages. All those contacts from the ICO. She enquires after their wives, families, corps.

'She is genuinely interested. You can see it in her face in a meeting. If someone else is speaking she'll give them 100% attention. You can see her face lighting up at what they say.'

Touch is important too. A firm handshake. Hand on the arm. Eye to eye contact. The kiss of greeting. A report on her visit to the Netherlands commented on the warmth of the greetings and wondered how many more kisses she could take. Her response would probably be 'Lots.' There is too much distance, not enough warmth and spontaneity in our 'civilised' world.

She still has a great sense of fun. She enjoys life, people, but is quick to see incongruities. Greeted by an 'explosion of applause' during one of her visits to America she quipped, 'After a welcome like that I can hardly wait to hear myself speak.' A cadet at the training college dressed up as General during an evening's light hearted entertainment. Within a couple of days Eva was repeating the jokes against herself to her office staff. Her old house mate, Helen, who hadn't appreciated the leaking roof at Howard met her on a trip to America.

'I did well training you to get you to this position,' she teased. Eva laughs as she tells the tale. Whatever situation she finds herself in she can handle. The 'brash Australian' still surfaces occasionally when she is excited about something. More often she is elegant, charming and totally in command.

'You can be confident that she will rise to any occasion. There is no time when you sit on the edge of your chair and think . . . oh.' Even when there is opposition those who are critical invariably end up eating out of her hand. Wherever she has gone in the world she has eased tension and raised spirits.

'She's good for morale,' said one officer. 'That can't be bad for any organisation, can it?'

She is also continuing to create a fair amount of media interest. Initially the fact of her being a woman was the novelty. Now it is more to do with personality. The easy rapport she has with those who interview her; the natural, unselfconscious approach. Her aim may be to give the Army publicity. Her lack of inhibitions ensure she achieves her objective. 'She enjoys every minute. She loves publicity. Loves being photographed. And knows exactly how she wants it done.' Just as she knows her own mind on other matters. Another fact which makes her newsworthy. A church leader with definite opinions and the dynamism to bulldoze her followers into some form of action is a rare breed.

After her election she stated she wanted to get things done. If her own record is anything to go by she is doing exactly that. She is in the office by 8am, has a daily meeting with her chief of staff at 9.30; the rest of the day is a constant stream of visitors, phone calls, interviews, letters, documents to sign, policies to discuss. Sometimes simultaneously. During one particularly fraught week in August she was doing the work of three leaders. Her own, her chief of staff (in a gap when one had retired and the other not yet taken up office) and that of a leader from the Central American area who was away sick. A congress in America gives some idea of the punishing schedule she is expected to maintain when she is away from her desk. Meetings at 8am, 10, 12.30, 2, 3, 4 and 7pm. General Burrows put in an appearance at most events despite jet lag, a difficult climate, and the press and TV pleading 'Squeeze us in. Please.'

Her diary must closely resemble that of members of the Royal family. In 1987 she led four zonal conferences in South Asia, the South Pacific and East Asia, Europe and Africa. She is expected to be preacher, chairperson, diplomat, pastor, administrator, guest, boss. You name it she does it.

In Britain the unemployment/social needs project is mainly her initiative. She will surely be keeping a keen eye on the church growth programme. Someone with such a positive personality finds the decline and lack of confidence which seem to have become endemic particularly hard to take.

Her agenda is daunting. There is little let up in the pressure. At International Headquarters there is always a 'hand behind your back' pushing relentlessly on. Surely there must be times when even a confirmed activist yearns 'Give me a break'? 'I take the days one at a time . . . With Jesus there were no panic measures. I want to be like that. Anyone who's a leader in today's world has to be able to cope with a very heavy diary.'

In fact not only does she cope, she appears to revel in it. Big assignments, action, people, coming up with ideas, seeing them implemented, all give her intense enjoyment. The biggest problem seems to be the expectation that everyone else can move at the same pace. Since she has arrived at IHQ she has definitely 'Set the cat among the pigeons. She has everyone running round in circles, wondering what's hit them. Especially the men.'

Her tremendous drive means she never seems to get tired, but doesn't always notice when everybody else does. She can do a morning's work, a two-hour question and answer session at the ICO, an interview in the car, and spend the evening preparing for a television appearance the next day. Any one of those activities could leave another person totally drained. Her staff appear to follow in her wake with a mixture of affection, exhaustion, admiration and exasperation. 'She is a workaholic. Without doubt. She works day and night.'

And weekends. And bank holidays. And annual leave. If she is not forcibly removed from her flat and the end of a telephone. That agile mind which can absorb the gist of a report at a preliminary glance is not going to turn off at the flick of a switch marked 'stop'. It can be hard for her staff, but they all have tremendous respect for her, and all that she is doing for the Army, and have found their own ways of coping.

So far she has been easing herself into the position. Finding her feet. Occupied in a public morale-lifting exercise. What she will do on the admin. side has yet to be seen, though there are hints in the kind of people she is appointing. They are not 'Yes men' but strong minded, with lots of ideas. People she respects and who respect her. Who will argue their case. General or not.

'I really am quite happy when someone contradicts me. That's one of the big disadvantages of leadership. You don't get people telling you what they really think. One of our American Commissioners once said, "The higher you go in the Salvation Army the more people talk about you and the less you know." I would like to feel that people weren't intimidated by my presence. I hope my open style would make them feel able to speak their mind. I admire a person who has strong convictions.'

Her emphasis is still very much on consultative leadership. She pledged at the High council to consult with four other leaders before selecting a new chief of staff, the chief executive who is left to do a lot of 'the hard grind of management'. In actual fact she consulted six. One of the things that makes her woman's leadership 'so acceptable' to men is her ability to listen to the views of her leaders. She may take some convincing if it is an issue on which she has strong opinions, but at least she will give them a hearing. 'She is genuinely looking for help and constructive ideas. She's very receptive of what other people think.'

Administration has never caused her any serious worries. If she's not sure about something, she asks. One of the first things she did at Headquarters was haul in the heads of each department so that she could get an understanding of the organisational side. She is definitely not the kind of boss who will creep into a building and nobody notice her. She wants to know what is going on. And why. And whether it can be improved. She chairs practically all the conferences and her knowledge is considered encyclopaedic. 'People may think I've got too much involvement but my style of leadership is not to control but encourage initiative. I have an awareness of what their work is about so most people around are on their toes all the time.'

If they're not, they need to watch out. She does not suffer fools gladly though she has infinite patience with those who have genuine difficulties. A girl came to interview her for radio. She had checked the recording machine before she left the studio. Everything appeared fine. When she came to do the interview it would not work. Despite her busy schedule Eva kept her cool. She too had once been let down by a temperamental machine. With the General of the day waiting for a timbrel display.

She is also a very caring person. News of the death or illness of officers or their wives always prompts a string of questions aimed at ensuring that everything possible is being done to meet their needs. 'She's got that touch with people. She doesn't make people feel she's far above them. If you invited her into your home she wouldn't expect an elaborate meal. She'd be quite happy to sit down in any old chair with a mug of coffee and be relaxed.' On the other hand she has high standards of efficiency in the office and there is very little she is afraid to tackle. If someone has to be dealt with her response is invariably 'Let's have them in and talk about it,' rather than waffling round the subject or passing the buck to someone else. The same applies when decisions are needed. 'There are times when you have to contemplate, meditate, but there are lots of things you can plough through, pass over. Unless it's something that's extremely problematical I say "Right. Let's do that".'

Then having decided the natural expectation is that everyone will fall in and follow the suggestion. Including the dignitaries at a civic dinner in Los Angeles where Eva had been talking about the Army's social work. To her the logical next step was a walk round Cardboard City to see the homeless folk for whom she was trying to raise funds. The dignitaries were none too pleased but they trailed after her. It takes a brave soul, such as an older sister, to stop someone as gifted as Eva Burrows in her tracks with a sharp 'You may think you're always right, but others are sometimes too.'

CHAPTER TWENTY FOUR

When Eva Burrows took office she was described as a 'formidable leader by any standards'. Salvationists throughout the world look on the General as a Father in God. She sees her leadership as a blend of spiritual authority and sanctified common sense. Any daughter of Ella Burrows would be well drilled in the latter; the spiritual demands are much greater cause for concern. Having hundreds of people hanging on your every word is a big responsibility and the physical and emotional demands of preaching can be very draining, especially when you pour your whole self into the activity as Eva does.

'I am always thrown back on the resources of God. When you are at the end of your own strength you lean so much more on God. The Holy Spirit seems to get hold of you in those times in such a way that afterwards you say, "Wasn't that amazing?" My human resources are limited, but God's resources are unlimited.'

Finding time for preparation is always problematic in such a demanding job. Eva has always found the book of Bible readings, the *Soldier's Armoury,* a good source of spiritual refreshment, though she regrets not having more time for reading and meditation. With so many decisions to make, so great a need for wisdom, she is constantly arrowing prayers for grace and guidance. To her life is prayer. Theresa of Avila is still a source of inspiration; the militant mystic whose 'Robust common sense, prudence and trust in Providence allied with an extraordinary capacity for work and organisation overcame all obstacles.' (*Oxford Dictionary of Saints*) The fact that she reformed the convents then set about sorting out the men is just cause for satisfaction though Eva no longer needs to sing 'Why can't a woman be more like a man?' She knows God can use male and female, rich and poor, old and young, and glories in the specific job God has given her to do. Others may see her as talented, gifted, a very capable lady. Her aim is always 'to please God', to seek his will and do it. Invariably this means applying her mind to a problem, clearing it of ulterior motives, and allowing the Holy Spirit to guide her. The incident at the High Council is still unique. She does not hear voices booming from the sky, whispers in her ear. Guidance is more likely to come through a focusing of thought, consensus of opinion, clarification of a situation, confirmation that a decision is right. Or occasionally wrong, and having the honesty to admit it.

'In my own spiritual life I suppose I'm trying to be more Christlike. Jesus Christ was a very attractive person. Holiness should not be a gloomy pietism but a goodness, a shining quality that draws people. When Jesus came near people they all wanted to be better.'

Her models are still 'shining people'. Catherine Bramwell Booth, granddaughter of the founder, who attracted the obituary 'A shining light' on her death at the age of 104. An Australian miner who when he sang 'Oh to be like Jesus' received the compliment 'I think you've made it, mate' from one of his workmates.

Getting the balance is difficult. Too many saintly people have their feet off the ground. Those who are down to earth often neglect their spiritual exercises. It takes a special person to have spiritual strength and good management skills.

'If she was a leader in any other career she would be a leader of some authority' commented one of Eva's staff. 'But spiritual authority is different. Because of her commitment and her own devotional practice she has the spiritual authority which belongs to anyone who has got their own spiritual life sorted out.'

When she is leading conferences and spiritual meetings people are amazed at the depth and sincerity. At the High Council she described the role of General as pastor, prophet, priest. The pastoral role comes naturally to someone who has always been fascinated by people. 'You show that in the care of the individuals who come within the orbit of your influence.'

The prophetic ministry has been far more significant than she ever imagined. Her own sense of inadequacy throws her constantly back on God, keeping the channels unblocked so his love can flow through. The role of priest has taught her new depths of intercessory prayer. In July 1987 she took a break in the Holy Land with Ingrid and Lucille Turfrey, a friend from Australia. During a week in Galilee they visited a chapel called Mensa Christi built on the spot claimed to be where Jesus told his disciple Peter 'Feed my sheep.' Inside the chapel is a great rock. Eva rested her head against its coolness thinking of Jesus, the Rock on whom she depended, and the flock, the Army, God had given her to feed. As she knelt she prayed for each leader of the Salvation Army in every country. She knew them all. Their names, faces, situations.

'I spent a little time in Nigeria, Congo, Ghana, Zaire, Zimbabwe. I went right through Africa, Asia . . . all the countries. I felt a great sense of Christ's presence at that moment.'

She knows if she had a partner and children to consider she would not be able to devote the same amount of time and energy to her task. She can, and does, give herself entirely to the Army. Apart from the occasional concert at the Barbican there is very little she does that is not Army oriented. 'Army-barmy' like her father perhaps?

'I am not so over-awed by the Army that I don't see its faults. There are many imperfections because it is run by imperfect human beings. There are many things you could criticise about the movement. We have made errors in the past and we will keep on making errors . . . but I believe this movement was called into being for a purpose. I'm very much committed to it. When I gave myself to Christ I had this strong conviction my place was in the Army. I sometimes say I have red, yellow and blue blood. The colours of our flag. Significant colours. So startling, so striking. Red for the blood of Christ. Blue for the holiness of God. Yellow for the fire of the Holy Spirit. Wherever I go in the world I see those colours.'

Flags, bands, firecrackers. Everybody's darling, but nobody's in particular. What of the loneliness of the top position? The sense of isolation that must inevitably come when the last person has eventually gone home, the chauffeur has delivered her to her apartment at the hotel, and the door closes on an empty room and a couple of suitcases?

Eva admits she needs to feel loved. Over the years she has disciplined herself to accept the fact that she cannot be near her family, but wherever she goes in the world she sends them postcards, articles, details of her itinerary. She hopes to spend Christmas in Australia with the family if it is possible. Friendships forged over the years with Ingrid, Miriam, Lucille Turfrey are a continuing strength despite the hundreds of miles between them most of the time. Her support team is invaluable. Mrs Groves, the chief of staff, her personal secretary, all who work closely with her and help form a protective net to keep her functioning on a daily basis.

She still misses the quiet gentleness of her younger sister. Those few weeks in Scotland and the time near one another in Australia were very precious. There is maybe a need for close trusted friends with whom she can share the deep things. Some substitute for the closeness of that central relationship which has not been possible. Though she can joke with her female staff that they have managed without men for so long now a few more years are not going to make a lot of difference. She is also realist enough to know that marriage is not always the partnership it was intended to be. Children can bring heartache as well as great joy as William Booth discovered. Besides, she is too much a 'people person' to wallow in loneliness or self pity. She sees singleness as a gift every bit as valuable as that of marriage. Pity the person who tries to patronise her for her single state. 'God gives more than enough back to you when you give up something for Him. He is nobody's debtor. You find your comfort and solace in Him.'

When she can pull herself to a halt sufficiently to spend time listening to what He is trying to tell her. 'That is my challenge personally. To spend time being a Mary. Jesus Christ is the centre of my life. Everything revolves round Him. But really to sit with Him. Then I'm thinking of something I should be doing for Him . . .'

She knows the dangers of activism; always being on the go, running ahead of God, asking his opinion after the event. The problem is putting a brake on that alert mind, harnessing the energy, conserving it. All she can do is bring herself, all that she is, back to the 'mercy seat'. Not in a public meeting necessarily. That would only cause a sensation and be counter productive, but quietly, continually, in the depths of her own heart.

'I've got my feet on the ground. I'm aware of my limitations. What I would be without the grace of God. I know even when I go in to preach I'm hanging on the Lord. I realise my vulnerability as a human being. I have to remind myself that my dependency is on God. You can be tempted.'

Pride is an obvious hazard for anyone in a leadership position, used to achieving, surrounded by admiring crowds. 'Keep her humble,' teases Helen, the American girl, who did her bit to 'take her down a peg or two' when they shared a hut in Africa. The warning does not fall on deaf ears. The young cadet who was so conscious of the fact that to 'those whom much has been given much will be required' now preaches on the same theme to the officers under her leadership. She knows that the gifts she has have come to her from her parents and from God. She must be very careful how she uses them.

Power does corrupt and as General of the Salvation Army she has a great deal of power. The only election the Army holds is that at the High Council to elect a General. There may be committees, consultation. The buck still stops at the big oak desk in the General's office on the first floor at International Headquarters. Whoever is in charge has the last word. The final decision. No one can stop them unless what they propose is illegal. It is a daunting thought. Is there no one to whom the General is answerable? Provision exists for the High Council to adjudicate on the fitness of a leader and remove them from office as Bramwell Booth so painfully experienced. Other than that it is a case of individual responsibility, and Eva Burrows is no stranger to that.

'All people who handle the things of God must be accountable. I see myself as being accountable to the Salvation Army and its principles. I see myself as being accountable to the people I lead, and most of all accountable to God.'

To her mind rules and regulations are not there to act as a sausage machine removing individuality, but to help produce disciplined soldiers capable of acting with a common purpose. The power she has been given is not that of dictator but servant. 'You can have power as Christ had power without being corrupted by it. The power of God is independent of intellect, or personality, or status. He had power with people rather than over people.'

She feels her own power comes very much from the strength she draws from God, and from the prayers of her people all round the world. From the letters that arrive on her desk and the conversations she has with people in many countries of the world she knows that people are praying for her regularly, daily. The General's photo occupies a prominent position on the wall of the citadel or living room from Birmingham to Burma. Even maybe one day behind the bamboo curtain. One of the thrills of her first year in office has been renewed contact with Chinese Salvationists.

The General may be the figurehead, the focus of attention. She cannot go it alone. A young officer recently out of Training College had grasped the essentials. 'We're all working towards the same aim. It's very evident with this General now. She's so one with the people. This is our aim. Where we're going.'

The hierarchies, structures, traditions may sometimes leave a lot to be desired. The benefits lie in the strong sense of loyalty, the ability to mobilise resources, the fact that individual purposes take second place to that of the movement. Eva Burrows believes that as in William Booth's day people still want someone to be their leader. She knows there are dangers. Manipulation. Self centredness. Self seeking. When she lectures her officers she is lecturing herself.

'A spiritual leader must live so close to God that the purpose of Christ is the priority, and not the self. Remember the verse of scripture "Seekest thou great things for thyself. Seek them not . . ."' When she works till midnight, one, two in the morning it is not so that people will say what a fantastic sermon, or wonder how she has had time to read and digest a detailed report. It is because that is the next job that needs to be done, and she is doing it. Even if it means going without her sleep. She says she can make do with six hours. Her staff doubt whether she gets that much. She is rarely in bed by midnight and is up again at six, singing, whistling, taking the housekeeper a cup of tea in bed. On an aeroplane journey her secretary may try to sneak a spy thriller onto her lap. If it works she gets absorbed. More likely papers and reports will take her attention. Those closest to her have learned to sit at a distance or let her get on with it. They know they need time to re-charge their batteries even if she doesn't.

Her energy is certainly remarkable. People talk of her tremendous stamina, vitality, the punishing pace she sets. The anxiety they sometimes feel. Though whether it is for her or themselves is not always clear. To some extent she is cushioned. Her immediate staff create a buffer, a back up system to take many of the every day chores. Cooking, driving, cleaning, secretarial work. The burden is still considerable. There are times when she could not stop, even if she wanted to. Fortunately she seems to take it all in her stride. She still sleeps so soundly she never remembers her dreams when she wakes. It is out of sleep and into action. No halfway stages. People who have worked with her over the years say they have never seen her depressed or tired though there are those who know when she has been overdoing it and find they need to practise some of the 'enabling grace' she sometimes preaches on. 'Nothing is impossible . . . our boss says so,' proclaims a poster on the wall of her outer office. Maybe it should be quoting her own words to her leaders in Australia?

'The spiritual leader is not immune from the operation of nature's laws. If he breaks the physical laws he will pay the physical penalty. You can't ask God Almighty to bless a seven-day week.'

CHAPTER TWENTY FIVE

'They'll probably tell you I've done too much. They do now. I can only live for God. Naturally as a General I mustn't live in a foolhardy way. The death of a General in office would be traumatic throughout the world. But my temperament's given to God, and I must live it out that way. I have a good friend who every time he sees me says "Don't forget. Pace yourself." It's difficult in this job, but I think I'm better at it.'

Energy, drive, the need for little sleep do seem to be significant factors in those who hold top leadership positions, but those who are constantly giving out also need time for taking in, refreshment. The holiday in the Holy Land was a good chance to unwind. Eva could almost walk out of her room into lake Galilee. 'I swam every day. Several days I swam at dawn with the sunrise coming over the Golan Heights, and the sun streaking the water. I loved that.'

Music is also playing an important part in her life again. She enjoys concerts at the Barbican, tapes and records she has not listened to for a long time. She can 'switch off' with a good book; though invariably she has a pencil at the ready to underline passages she can use as illustrations in her next preaching engagement. At home she is relaxed, easy, pleasant, considerate. She often asks Beth Groves 'Why don't you put your feet up?' Mrs Groves has a ready answer, 'Why don't you?'

She still watches her diet, but enjoys her food, especially soups which are not such are regular part of the culinary scene in a hot country like Australia. When banquets and rich foods are difficult to avoid Mrs Groves adjusts her menus to make sure the cholesterol contents are not too high in the meals Eva eats at home. The doctor recently gave her a clean bill of health. It is seven years since the heart attack. She is now no more at risk than the rest of the population. So long as she abides by the rules.

After a day at the desk she enjoys doing a few practical chores. Washing up, arranging flowers, making the coffee, or a dessert if they are entertaining. The young officer who 'excelled' at making cakes with the simplest ingredients in Africa, and snipped the stalks of flowers with her teeth has not forgotten the basic homemaking skills. She still has no fixed abode, though her present apartment high above the walls of the City of London once belonged to Benazir Bhutto. Eva delights to tell how they still occasionally get phone calls for her. The standard reply is 'This flat's not got politics now. It's got religion.'

She no longer sleeps four to a mattress on old apple crates, but the Van Gogh posters and aboriginal oil painting still hang on the wall. The dusky pink and light grey furniture and coverings speak style, and simplicity but old habits die hard. The first thing she does when she comes through the door is kick off her shoes, though the surviving Burrows children no longer have to walk barefoot or rely on charity for essential items. They all have good jobs and lovely homes. Eva is probably the poorest in the family in financial terms but she has no intention of letting it worry her. She can still live 'very simply' and is used to any excess earnings being paid direct to the Salvation Army. In Africa her teachers salary went straight to the organisation. Now it is more likely to be money from books, articles, television interviews. Her basic 'allowance' is probably little higher than a corps officer with a couple of children, and would make the hair of other heads of international organisations stand on end. As long as there is sufficient she is content. 'I think money's functional. To expend something to save my time that's a valuable use. Then I can spend my energies on other things.'

A family photo shows Eva, aged eleven, standing with her parents and brothers and sisters. They make a striking bunch. 'You can see there she's full of life. Look at her eyes,' says Beth Groves. 'And she was only a youngster then.'

Fifty years on her eyes are still her most striking feature. They light at talk of the Army's triumphs, its ministry worldwide, new initiatives like the AIDS project in Zambia. Deepen as she talks of sickness in her own family circle, or the death of leaders like Commissioner Samuel, one of their gifted and prominent Indian leaders who had sat with her in the garden of Sunbury Court under a flowering almond tree and told her 'Your becoming General is like a springtime in the Salvation Army.'

The demands of the job are considerable. Compared to those faced by the apostle Paul, another of her heroes, she feels they are nothing. He had to face opposition, critisism, misunderstanding, defections as he worked to establish the young churches. She has a loyal Army of soldiers. The back-up of her support team. The love of her international 'family'. God's continuing strength. She enjoys her work, enjoys being General. Being a woman has certainly not been a handicap. 'It has caused a great deal more public interest and given the Army more opportunities.'

She will not be easy to follow but if her successor is a man, as it undoubtedly will be, he will have a ready-made excuse. General Burrows had an unfair advantage. Meanwhile she will just get on with the job, rejecting labels such as motherly or maternal, unsuspecting journalists heap on her indignant head. She has warmth. She is a caring person. But above all she is highly professional. Everything she does is of her best. It always has been and as long as she has strength it always will be. She talks about the 'givenness' of leadership. The skills, the natural ability, the charisma, the creativity are all qualities which have been given. It is her responsibility to use them.

Nearly sixty years ago Robert Burrows dedicated his

newly born eighth child to 'the salvation of the world'. Her whole adult life has been given to exactly that purpose. 'I've come to feel almost from my mother's womb that God's hand was on my life,but since I've been in this office I've really felt God's hand heavy on me.'

Even her period of disobedience as a teenager has been turned to good. It gives her an appreciation of the rebelliousness of youth, the need everyone has to come to their own decision about the direction their life is to take. The time at social services would not have been her natural choice. Looking back she is grateful for that experience. It all helps to reinforce her view that such things should be taken as from God and that God can use them to work out His purposes. Hers is not a fatalistic view of destiny but a consciousness of God's love controlling, guiding, directing. The inexperienced graduate on the deck of the *Otranto* who was so used to being the centre of attention is still very much the leader, but far more conscious of how her life constantly needs to be under the direction and discipline of God.

The pressures of the job alone are sufficient to 'keep her humble', ensure she stays dependent. The sight of security forces guarding her route in Zimbabwe and knowledge of the knife edge she walks when she is outspoken on certain political and socio-moral issues must make her doubly so. To say nothing of minor incidents like a piece of the wing falling off the aeroplane and forcing a return to Heathrow when she was scheduled to meet the President of the United States.

Whatever the future may hold Eva feels that she has had 'an extraordinarily rich life in terms of international experience'. In 1991 she will have been an officer for forty years. That year also sees the end of her official term in office though there is provision on Orders and Regulations for an extension up to three years beyond. She may not be able to go 'on and on' like the lady at Westminster half a mile or so up-stream, but she will certainly make the most of whatever time she has. Already her staff threaten to 'put glue on her seat' when she is off on a major assignment. The prospect of trying to wind her down when retirement looms on the horizon is not one they care to contemplate. When she had to let go of Africa it left an enormous gap in her life. What will happen when the time comes to bow out gracefully from the top job? The idealist with no illusions has already looked that squarely in the face.

'It must be difficult to stop. Wean yourself from work. You must feel bereft initially but I would ask for grace to let go when the time comes. I think women are pretty good at retirement.' Not that she has any intention of sitting in a sheltered cottage knitting. 'I might travel. Go back and see places as a tourist. I would be very happy to go back to Africa. Take an assignment/duty there. I could go back to university and do a theology degree. Batchelor of Divinity. I wanted to do it when I was teaching in Africa but I didn't have the time. Retired Generals are often asked to a lot of preaching. It would be lovely to have time for proper preparation. Whatever I do it will be an active retirement.'

Obviously. If studying or preaching are not on the agenda she would love to paint. 'If I get that far. If I don't burn myself out before then.' She looks you straight in the eye. Defiantly. As she has already outfaced 'the last enemy'. Like Commissioner Catherine and her own mother, Eva Burrows is 'in love with life' and has no intention of handing it over without a fight. Whatever the joys to follow.

'I have a positive outlook about life beyond this one. I believe we'll have such tremendous spiritual and intellectual development that if I haven't finished my thesis for the Doctor of Divinity I'll continue . . . We don't know how it will be but I think it's going to be a place of great growth.'

Meanwhile she is a Methusalite, a person who believes in living as long as possible, and enjoying every minute; as she did on board the *Ontranto* watching the lights of London twinkling in the distance; as she did in Africa teaching and training the people of an emerging nation; as she does now as General of an international Army.

She is no little tin god but 'an ordinary sort of person' who will take a suggestion from a child's letter and use it in the planning of a major meeting. She has no illusions about the status of her Army in the eyes of the world or other Christians. She knows it is viewed as a minority organisation, bottom of the denominational pile, more bands than brains. It might be useful for shifting butter mountains, but in Britain, its birthplace, is often treated with amused tolerance by those who do not have to sleep in a cardboard box or rely on the Army for a meal when the social security offices are closed or unable to help.

Providing she is in the right place, where God wants, Eva will leave the only judgement that really matters to God. She has kept her promise and used what God has given her well. She sang an Army hymn during a time of worship on that holiday in Galilee. It could have summarised her whole life.

My life must be Christ's broken bread,
My love his outpoured wine,
A cup o'er filled, a table spread,
Beneath his name and sign,
That other souls refreshed and fed
May share his life through mine.

Other Marshall Pickering Paperbacks

RICH IN FAITH

Colin Whittaker

Colin Whittaker's persuasive new book is written for ordinary people all of whom have access to faith, a source of pure gold even when miracles and healing seem to happen to other people only.

The author identifies ten specific ways to keep going on the road to faith-riches, starting where faith must always begin—with God himself, the Holy Spirit, the Bible, signs and wonders, evangelism, tongues and finally to eternal life with Christ.

OUR GOD IS GOOD

Yonggi Cho

This new book from Pastor Cho describes the blessings, spiritual and material, that reward the believer. Yonggi Cho presents his understanding of the fullness of salvation, bringing wholeness to God's people.

HEARTS AFLAME
Stories from the Church of Chile

Barbara Bazley

Hearts Aflame is a book suffused with love for the large, sometimes violent country of Chile and joy at the power of the Gospel taking root.

Each chapter is a story in itself, telling of some encounter, episode of friendship that has left its mark on the author's life.

THE PLIGHT OF MAN AND THE POWER OF GOD

Dr Martin Lloyd-Jones

The text of the highly esteemed sermons given by Dr Martin Lloyd-Jones, based on verses from Romans, Chapter One, focuses on our need to be entirely committed to the Christian gospel.

Dr Lloyd-Jones highlights the uniqueness of the faith. Because of this he stresses the necessity of our absolute commitment to Christ and his call to us.

This book will be of great interest to all thoughtful Christians and of help to preachers, speakers and students.

THE NATURAL TOUCH

Kim Swithinbank

Some people think of 'evangelism' as knocking on doors, reading your Bible on the train or starting up conversations with strangers in which you get on to the four-point-plan-of salvation as quickly as possible. Some of these activities we would do, others we'd cringe at doing.

In his first book, Kim Swithinbank says that sharing our hope in Christ is something that we are *all* asked to do. It should be as natural as breathing to us.

Taking us through the most common obstacles which keep people away from Christianity, he shows how we can develop a lifestyle which is attractive and compelling for Christ.

Kim Swithinbank is Director of Evangelism at All Souls, Langham Place.

If you wish to receive *regular information* about *new books*, please send your name and address to:

London Bible Warehouse
PO Box 123
Basingstoke
Hants RG23 7NL

Name..

Address ....

....

....

....

I am especially interested in:

- ☐ Biographies
- ☐ Fiction
- ☐ Christian living
- ☐ Issue related books
- ☐ Academic books
- ☐ Bible study aids
- ☐ Children's books
- ☐ Music
- ☐ Other subjects